THE STORY OF PAUL

THE EARLY YEARS.

THE STORY OF PAUL

THE EARLY YEARS.

BY TREVOR GALPIN

Copyright ©2018

The Story of Paul - The Early Years
by Trevor Galpin
Published by TLG Mins

Design & Layout by Tom Carroll

Printed by CreateSpace a division of Amazon

ISBN: 978-0-9575318-9-5

All rights reserved. No part of this publication may be reproduced, stored in a retrieval system or transmitted in any form or by any means - for example, electronic, photocopy, recording - without the prior written permission of the author or publisher. The only exception is brief quotation in printed reviews.

All Scripture quotations, unless otherwise indicated, are taken from The Holy Bible, New International Version®, NIV® Copyright ©1973, 1978, 1984, 2011 by Biblica, Inc.®. Used by permission.
All rights reserved worldwide.

For more information and resources by Trevor and Linda, please visit:
www.trevorlindafhm.com

CONTENTS

	Foreword	VII
	Preface	X
	Map of the area in the first Century AD.	XIII
I.	The Prisoner.	1
II.	The Pharisee.	8
III.	The Encounter on the Road to Damascus.	26
IV.	The Follower of the Way.	51
V.	The Place of Revelation.	63
VI.	The Return to Jerusalem.	76
VII.	The Teacher in Antioch.	84
VIII.	The Church Planter.	96
IX.	The Council of Jerusalem.	111
X.	The Lone Voice.	127
XI.	The Letter Writer.	136
XII.	The Son and Heir.	151
	Epilogue	169
	Reading List & Other Books by Trevor Galpin	173

FOREWORD

The apostle Paul is probably the most influential person in human history next to Jesus Christ. Jesus opened a door that Paul walked through 'seeing' and 'learning' things that he was able to pass on to the world in a way that Jesus was unable to do. We read Jesus' words telling us he was unable at that time to do this in John 12:16,

"I still have many things to say to you, but you cannot bear them now. However, when he, the Spirit of truth, has come, he will guide you into all truth; for he will not speak on his own authority, but whatever he hears he will speak; and he will tell you things to come."

When the Spirit came upon the apostle Paul, he became able to 'see' and communicate truth to an extent that no one else had ever been able to do before. Jesus of course knew it, but he gave it to Paul to communicate it.

Essentially what the apostle Paul wrote in his letters to the churches was a large contribution of the continuation of Jesus' teaching that people were unable to 'hear' when Jesus was walking the earth.

Paul was therefore a very significant Christian teacher, probably the most significant of all. Paul said several times in his many letters

FOREWORD

that we should be imitators of him, which no other writer of the New Testament ever asked. There are more lessons of a personal nature in Paul's writings of how he lived his life as a follower of Jesus Christ than any other New Testament writer. He is our shining light of how to be a follower of Jesus Christ. We need to note these things very well and learn from the great apostle Paul as much as we can.

In this very easy to read, informative and entertaining book by my friend, brother and fellow servant of the Body of Christ, Trevor Galpin, you will be introduced to Paul in a deeper and more full way than I have ever known to be in print. Trevor's detailed knowledge of Paul's life and the historical setting of his day is mixed with a well-informed imagination. Trevor builds pictures and insights into the events of Paul's life and the deep perspectives that Paul held in his heart, forming his way of walking in Christ Jesus.

Paul wrote to the Corinthians that Timothy, Paul's son in the Lord, knew not only the revelations and teachings that Paul carried and presented to the churches he planted, visited and watered in the early church, but Timothy also knew Paul's ways in Christ. In 1 Corinthians 4:17, Paul says,

> *"For this reason I have sent Timothy to you, who is my beloved and faithful son in the Lord, who will remind you of my ways in Christ, as I teach everywhere in every church."*

In this book, Trevor has searched deeply into the writings of Paul's letters to bring out the deeper things of Paul's personal life and uncover what exactly made the apostle Paul tick. What was the background of this amazing man? How did he see being a disciple of Jesus, a slave of Christ, a servant of the Body of Christ? What did being a Christian mean to him? Who was the man we esteem so much? And how can we follow in Paul's footsteps as fellow followers of Christ?

Christianity has many expressions all over the world today, and there are such differences across the gamut of those expressions that some of them have little resemblance to each other. But Jesus and his disciples, including Paul the one born out of timing with the others, were united and wrote one book together which we call the New Testament. They were inspired of God with a unity of agreement in their writings that is supernatural.

Let this book draw us all back to the centre, source and life-giving wellspring of God who in Jesus unites us as sons and daughters in the Family of God.

James Jordan
Taupo, New Zealand, 2018

PREFACE

Why another book on the apostle Paul? Haven't there been enough books on him already? Here is why.

The apostle Paul has been with me all my Christian life. What I mean by that is, my earliest memory of the apostle was being informed by my parents that my middle name was Paul and I was named after him. I had no idea what they were talking about. Much later, I discovered what they meant. They were expressing in some way their hopes for me, that I would be like Paul. Whatever the reason behind it, I have always had some sort of affinity with the apostle. That was about as far as it went for years. In the 1970s, I studied theology at Spurgeon's College and whilst Paul was on the curriculum, he was not a major focus for me. In many ways, I felt more akin to the apostle Peter in his ups and downs. Incidentally, my brother had Peter as his middle name. The apostle Peter had an opinion about Paul also, one that I shared. He says of Paul in his second letter.

> "... Our dear brother Paul also wrote you with the wisdom that God gave him. He writes the same way in all his letters, speaking in them of these matters. His letters contain some things that are hard to understand..." (2 Peter 3:16).

PREFACE

That just about summed up my opinion of Paul. There was a lot in Paul that was hard to understand. My interests in theological college went into the realm of Church History. Later as a local church pastor, I would preach from Paul's letters but often majored on what I felt were the practical sections, usually towards the end of each letter, rather than what I thought were the heavy bits. However, over the last few years, I have personally discovered truth that I had not really seen before in the New Testament. I began to receive revelation that God is a Father who wants us to know and be known intimately by him. This has changed my whole perspective on what it is to be a Christian and a son of God. I have written about that in my first book *Falling from grace into Grace and being caught by the Father*.

What has also happened as I continue this journey is I have rediscovered Paul the apostle and found that he had an amazing revelation of God in Christ. I keep revisiting the writings of Paul in his letters and discovering things I had never seen before. They are truly a gold mine of truth. This led me to think about how Paul received such incredible revelation and the battles he had to fight to share this truth with us.

In this book about Paul, I imagine how these events unfolded and how he received this revelation.

Inevitably, I cannot write about these things just from a theological point of view. I am not wired like that. I wanted to know what Paul was like. Why he said the things he said. More to the point, I wanted to see how the legalistic Jewish Pharisee who persecuted the early church was transformed into the man who had a profound revelation of the love of God the Father expressed in and through Jesus Christ his beloved Son. I want to tell his story as it appears in the pages of the New Testament. I want also to get behind the

PREFACE

words and meet the man.

One of the challenges is how to refer to him. For the first part of the story, he is called by his Aramaic or perhaps Jewish name Saul and only becomes known as Paul at the beginning of his first missionary journey while on the island of Cyprus. In all his letters, he refers to himself as Paul, and I have attempted to follow that pattern up to the time Saul changed his name to Paul.

Our primary source of information about Paul comes from the account written in the New Testament by Luke in the work known as the Acts of the Apostles. There are also bits and pieces of biographical information scattered through the thirteen letters attributed to Paul, and my fertile imagination has pieced the story together from these sources.

What conversations went on? What was the back story? Who were the people Paul worked with and knew? Though this is not a novel, from time to time it has been necessary to conjecture a little about how the various events were linked. Therefore, in writing this nonfiction work, I closely follow the events as they unfold in the New Testament and here and there, I imagine what people were thinking and saying weaving a historical narrative into the text. I think it will be self-evident when that happens. I also wanted to explore Paul's revelation and teaching as these have deeply impacted me, and I believe they are a word for the whole Church today.

I believe Paul saw things with the eyes of his heart that very few have seen, and he has much to teach us. I also believe it is a jolly good cracking story to tell!

Trevor Galpin
United Kingdom, 2018

THE EASTERN END OF THE MEDITERRANEAN SEA AND THE ROMAN EMPIRE IN THE FIRST CENTURY AD.

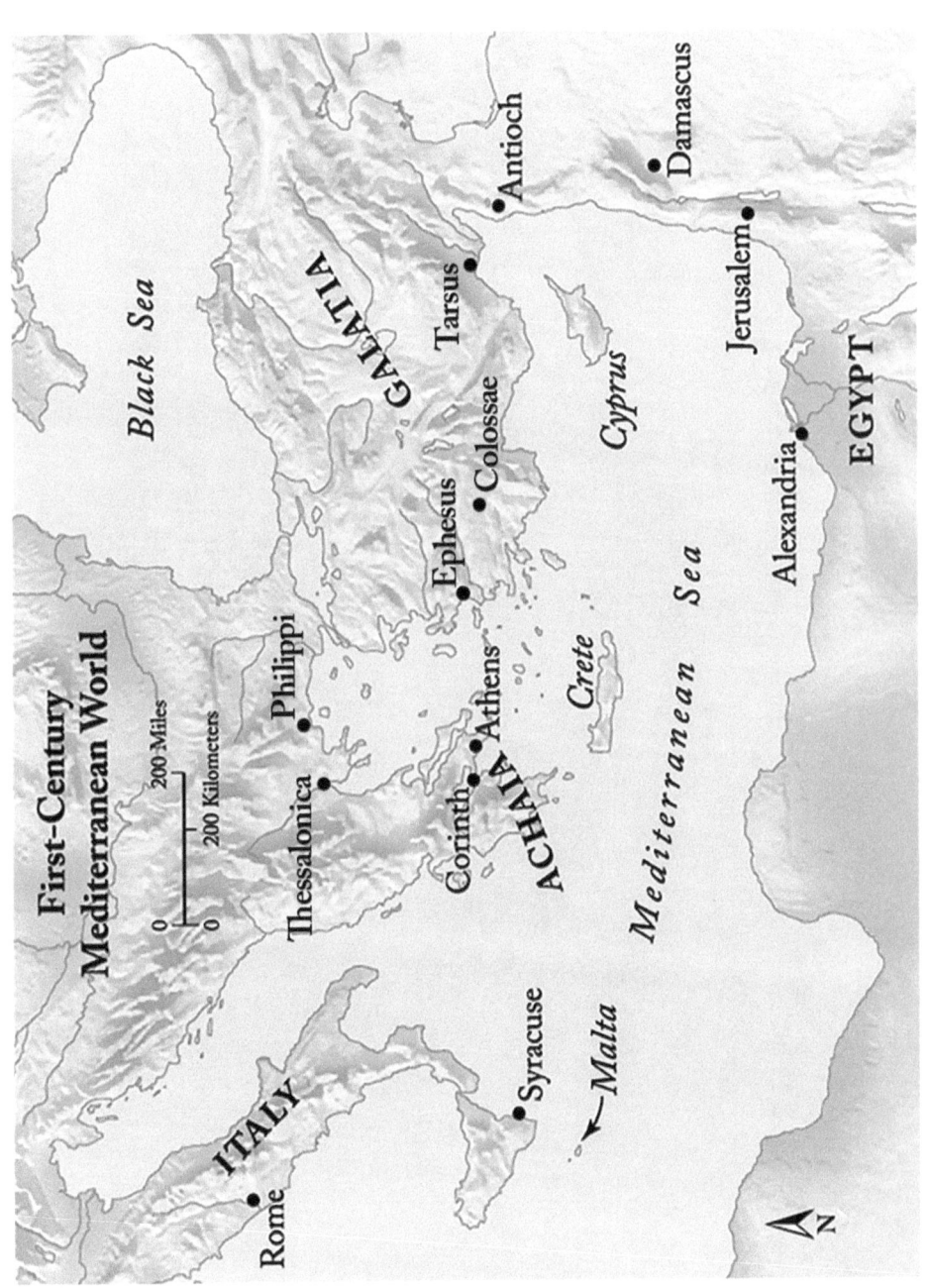

CHAPTER I

THE PRISONER.

*T*he prisoner stood before them chained hand and foot. He was a short man, and his age was a difficult thing to determine. Hair thin and lank, his balding head was scarred. Age lines framed the eyes of his pale face. Two years of incarceration had leached the tan of his travels out of his skin, turning it into a pallid paste that highlighted the scars of frequent beatings. His nose was bent and hooked and appeared to have been broken and healed a number of times. The prisoner's eyes were red like flames as he struggled to focus on the people in front of him. For years, he had suffered with eye infections and poor eye sight. Now, after being kept so long in a dark cell, they burned and stung in the bright light of the audience chamber of the governor's palace. The fetid stink of prison clung to his threadbare tunic, invading the space of those nearby. One of the guards wrinkled his nose and shifted sideways to distance himself from the miasma.

The prisoner was Paul also known by his Jewish name, Saul of Tarsus.

∿∿∿

Paul stood slightly stooped and raised his head to look up at the assembled group of dignitaries arrayed before him like classical Greek actors in the theatre of his home town, Tarsus. In the centre, occupying the seat of honour, sat Marcus Julius Agrippa. He was

CHAPTER I

the great grandson of the last of the Jewish kings to have ruled over the whole of the Roman province of Judaea, King Herod the Great. The first Herod had been king when Jesus was born in Bethlehem. The man whom Paul stood before this day was styled King Herod Agrippa II. In reality, his authority amounted to very little, but his prestige came from being a survivor and a close friend of the Emperor Claudius. Most of his relatives in the dynasty of Herod the Great had died of mysterious circumstances or deliberately murdered in family feuds. He and Claudius were both survivors. Through political manoeuvring and fox-like cunning, which was a family trait, Agrippa had survived. After the death of Claudius and the accession to the imperial thrown of the totally insane and brutal Caligula and then the notorious Nero, Agrippa had survived.

Next to him sat his sister Julia Berenice. To describe her as sitting would be inaccurate. She was draped across the chair beside her brother leaning towards him in a less than sisterly way. The rumours about their relationship were the talk of the aristocracy and the subject of graffiti on the walls of brothels in Caesarea. Her reputation had even reached the ears of the Jewish historian Josephus. Bernice, as she was also known, was a survivor in a world where aristocratic women were treated like toys and chattels. Ever since the days when Queen Cleopatra beguiled Julius Caesar and Mark Antony, Eastern princesses with their unique brand of exotic mystery were of particular interest to Roman aristocracy. Bernice was no different, and she was noted for her dalliances.

Alongside these two sat the newly appointed Roman governor of the province, Porcius Festus.

A few days earlier, King Agrippa and Bernice had arrived in Caesarea to pay their respects, and Festus took the opportunity to discuss the prisoner Paul. Festus had inherited this issue from his predecessor Marcus Antonius Felix. Felix, a corrupt and evil man married to Drusilla, the youngest daughter of Agrippa I and the sister of Agrippa II and Bernice, was keen to make money out of his position as the Roman procurator of Judea.

Two years earlier after an absence of some years, Paul and a group of friends had arrived back in Jerusalem and were enjoying the opportunity to be in the temple precincts performing various purifications rituals over several days. Luke, one of Paul's travelling companions, records the events in detail in Acts chapter 21 and 22. Towards the end of this purification process, Paul was recognised by a group of Jews from the Roman province of Asia. They accused him of defiling the temple by bringing Gentiles into the precincts and being a blasphemer who taught against their law. In the commotion that followed, they attacked him and had beat him almost to the point of death when Captain of the Guard, Lysias intervened and discovered Paul was a Roman citizen. Lysias took him into custody for his own safety, and various hearings were held involving the Jewish religious leaders when a plot to kill him emerged.

After Paul's arrest, forty Jewish men bound themselves in an oath to abstain from eating or drinking until they killed Paul. The Jewish leaders agreed to help them by petitioning the Roman commander to bring Paul before the Sanhedrin for questioning. The assassins planned to attack Paul during the transfer. However, the son of Paul's sister heard of the plot and reported it to him at the Roman barracks. When Paul told a centurion, the Roman commander ordered a detachment of almost five hundred guards move him to Caesarea under the cover of night.

Luke records that the soldiers, carrying out their orders, took Paul with them during the night and brought him as far as Antipatris. The next day, they let the cavalry go on with him, while they returned to the barracks. When the cavalry arrived in Caesarea, they delivered a letter to the governor and handed Paul over to him. The governor read the letter and asked what province Paul was from. Learning that he was from Cilicia, he said, "I will hear your case when your accusers get here," and ordered that Paul be kept under guard in Herod's palace (Acts 23:31-35).

The Governor Felix presided over the first trial of Paul, which took place in Caesarea in about 56 AD. This occurred within a few days of Paul's being brought to Caesarea. Several members of the Sanhedrin, the high priest, and their spokesman Tertullus appeared before Felix. The Sanhedrin, or more properly the Great Sanhedrin, was the supreme council of the Jews composed of seventy elders plus the high priest. The Great Sanhedrin, who met daily in Jerusalem's temple, had jurisdiction over religious matters. They were the ones who arrested, tried, and condemned Jesus to death. Before this body, Paul was accused of profaning the temple and agitating all the Jews throughout the world. Felix had the presence of mind to allow Paul to speak in his own defence. Essentially, Paul said the council had no proof and that it would simply be their word against his. Felix decided to wait for the arresting officer, Lysias, to come to Caesarea to provide impartial information. For some reason, Lysias never came and Paul was not released.

Felix permitted Paul's friends to visit him in prison in the palace at Caesarea and take care of his needs. Without these liberties, Paul undoubtedly would have died in prison. Periodically, Felix and his wife sent for Paul. According to Luke, Felix was hoping Paul would offer him a bribe. When Felix was relieved of his duties in 58 AD, he had still not settled Paul's case, so Paul languished in prison for the next two years.

Porcius Festus had been appointed by the Emperor Nero as the next governor and went to Jerusalem upon his arrival to meet the Jewish leaders. They immediately asked him to extradite Paul back to Jerusalem to stand trial on their previous charges. Their intention was to kill Paul on the way. Festus had only been in office a few days, at this point, so he tried to buy himself some time, saying he would be returning to Caesarea shortly and would take up the issue at that time.

Festus arrived in Caesarea and reopened Paul's case. The Jews had no more evidence two years after the fact than they previously had. It was still a matter of Paul's word versus theirs. According to Luke's account, apparently, they never worked on gathering any real evidence because they had always intended to assassinate Paul. Festus decided the highest Jewish ruling body, the Sanhedrin, would be a more appropriate venue than a Roman court to deal with the issue since it was obviously a religious matter and not a political one. He asked Paul if he would be willing to go to Jerusalem to face his accusers.

Paul knew he would never get a fair trial in Jerusalem and appealed to Caesar, a right granted to Roman citizens. "Appealing to Caesar" was rarely done, but it was allowed by law. To go to Rome was very expensive and rarely did the emperor disavow a previous decision, however in this case, no decision had been granted, therefore Festus had no choice but to grant Paul's request. Provincial governors were not likely to send petty cases before Caesar and usually handled such matters locally, but Festus was quite new at his post and had no interest in portraying himself as incompetent. He needed to write a letter of explanation to Caesar but found himself at a loss for words.

To Festus' great delight, Agrippa II and his sister, Bernice came to pay a state visit to meet the new governor in Caesarea, and he decided to explain to them how he had inherited this messy case.

CHAPTER I

Festus told them the whole convoluted story, saying Paul's accusers had some points of dispute with him about their own religion and about a dead man named Jesus whom this prisoner claimed was alive. Festus said he was at a loss how to investigate such matters and added that he thought the evidence against Paul was weak, but when the prisoner appealed to be held over for the Emperor's decision, he ordered Paul to be held until he could send him to Caesar.

Upon hearing all this, Agrippa decided he wanted to hear this man himself. Most likely, Festus was delighted and relieved to have someone who might able to resolve the case.

As a result, the next day Paul was brought before the authorities. Agrippa and Bernice came with great pomp, entering the audience room with the high-ranking military officers and the prominent men of the city.

Festus addressed the gathered group dignitaries and officials.

"King Agrippa, and all who are present with us, you see this man! The whole Jewish community has petitioned me about him in Jerusalem and here in Caesarea, shouting that he ought not live any longer. I found he had done nothing deserving of death, but because he made his appeal to the Emperor, I decided to send him to Rome though I have nothing definite to write to His Majesty about him. Therefore, I have brought him before all of you, and especially before you, King Agrippa, so that as a result of this investigation, I may have something to write. For I think it is unreasonable to send a prisoner on to Rome without specifying the charges against him."

Agrippa then said to Paul, "You have permission to speak for yourself" (Acts 25:24 - 26:1).

Every eye in the great hall of judgement turned and looked at the diminutive figure standing in chains in the centre. Before these gathered dignitaries stood a towering spiritual giant of a man, Paul the apostle, Saul of Tarsus. This was Paul, the great revealer of truth, one of the greatest minds the world has known.

In perhaps his greatest moment with his most significant audience he had addressed up to that time, Paul was about to tell his story in his own words. Every thought would be crafted in his brilliant mind before being uttered. Every word would be carefully chosen. Every pause pregnant with meaning. Every gesture adding effect. His voice, his tone, his passion would resonate through every sentence.

Paul motioned with his hand and began his defence:

"King Agrippa, I consider myself fortunate to stand before you today as I make my defence against all the accusations of the Jews, and especially so because you are well acquainted with all the Jewish customs and controversies. Therefore, I beg you to listen to me patiently. The Jewish people all know the way I have lived ever since I was a child, from the beginning of my life in my own country, and also in Jerusalem. They have known me for a long time and can testify, if they are willing, that I conformed to the strictest sect of our religion, living as a Pharisee. And now it is because of my hope in what God has promised our ancestors that I am on trial today. This is the promise our twelve tribes are hoping to see fulfilled as they earnestly serve God day and night. King Agrippa, it is because of this hope that these Jews are accusing me" (Acts 26:2-7).

Paul the prisoner began his story with his early life and upbringing as a Pharisee.

CHAPTER II

THE PHARISEE.

*T*he young man pushed his way forward to the front of the crowd. Many of the men around him, he knew well and had spent many hours studying and debating with them. They were as passionate as he about their holy book, the Torah. He had read it so many times, studied it, and reread it. He knew its Hebrew by heart, every jot and tittle. He could recite page after page. As conversant with its Greek translation, the Septuagint, as he was the original Hebrew, he prided himself that he was of the tribe of Benjamin, a Hebrew of the Hebrews. No one could surpass him in the depth of his knowledge or his zeal for the Law.

His birth in Tarsus and his inherited Roman citizenship added a sophistication to his whole demeanour, and he loved to associate with other young intellectuals and scholars like himself. Their meeting place in Jerusalem, the Synagogue of the Freedmen as it was called, was his favourite haunt to debate and argue minute points of the Mosaic law. Most of the young men were from the provinces where there were many Hellenistic Jews like him, provinces such as Asia, Alexandria, Cyrene and Cilicia, his home province. Saul of Tarsus was not some peasant from Galilee. He was told by many that he was destined for great things. Perhaps one day there would be a rabbinical school named after him such as had been given to his teacher and mentor, the great Gamaliel ben Hillel.

Yet, this day had been diffcrent. A young Greek speaking Jew had turned up and an argument had started about some of his beliefs. He was clearly not orthodox and as the argument heated up, it became apparent that he was one of the loathed new sect that had been troubling everyone in the city for many months. Finally, it was too much for some of them, and they seized this man named Stephenos, plotting to have him arrested and accused of blasphemy.

They dragged Stephenos to the High Priest where he could be heard and tried. The whole group was very excited. They arrived at the great hall where the Sanhedrin was already assembled, seated in a large semicircle. Saul recognised many of the old and venerable men gathered there. As the crowd filled the hall, an official called for silence and the room fell quiet. The air was thick with dust from the streets swept in by the crowd. A heaviness and tension pervaded the atmosphere. One by one, accusations were made against Stephenos. When the last person spoke, they all turned and looked at the accused. From his position in the front row, Saul stared at the man. He looked serene; there was no fear or apprehension in the man's eyes. One of the old men on the council, his head covered by his prayer shawl, leaned forward and said he thought he saw the face of an angel. The young men laughed in derision and again there was a call for silence. The High Priest raised his hand and pointed at Stephenos, "Are these things true?"

Stephenos began to speak. Sweat rolled down Saul's back in the stifling heat of the crowded hall as he listened intently. Each sentence pierced the atmosphere. Every word Stephenos uttered, Saul knew added fuel to the fire that was burning in each person listening. Saul's anger rose within him as he heard the man quote stories from the Holy Book. The inference Stephenos made was not lost on any of them when he said,

"You stiff-necked people! Your hearts and ears are still uncircumcised. You are just like your ancestors: You always resist the Holy Spirit! Was there ever a prophet

CHAPTER II

your ancestors did not persecute? They even killed those who predicted the coming of the Righteous One. And now you have betrayed and murdered him, you who have received the law that was given through angels but have not obeyed it" (Acts 7:51-53).

It was too much, and the whole assembly began to roar and shout. A number of the elders stood up and tore their priestly robes as a sign of their contempt. Amid the din, a voice rose louder than the others. It was Stephenos.

"Look," he said, "I see heaven open and the Son of Man standing at the right hand of God." At this some of them covered their ears and, yelling at the top of their voices, they all rushed at him, dragging him out of the city.

Saul ran along with them, and it became apparent that Stephenos was doomed. Men were picking up stones and rocks from the side of the road. He was taken outside the city gate and thrown on the ground against the city wall. The first stone hit him on his leg. Other well aimed rocks were launched from the crowd. Men began to take off their cloaks and outer coats as they stoned him in the heat. Saul reached out and piled their coats at his feet, watching the spectacle. To ensure maximum pain was inflicted before the victim lost consciousness, rocks were carefully aimed to avoid the head. There was a pause, then Saul heard Stephenos pray out loud.

"Lord Jesus, receive my spirit."

Then he fell on his knees and cried out,

"Lord, do not hold this sin against them."

When he had said this, a well-aimed stone hit him full in the face followed by a rain of others at the head. It was all over, and the crowd laughed and chatted as they returned into the city. Saul stood there brooding, staring at the bloody mass of broken bones and flesh. After *a little while, a few men came forward and retrieved the body of the dead youth. Saul looked at them, mentally marking their faces into his memory. "They will be next," he thought as he went back into the city.*

∿∿∿

According to the Acts of the Apostles, Saul was born in Tarsus. He was a Jew by birth and part of the Diaspora, the word used to describe the spread of the Jewish people across the Roman and Greek world that had begun several hundred years before. Proud of his heritage and the city of his birth, he was known by his Jewish name Saul of Tarsus in his early days. When arrested by the Roman commander, he told him he was a Jew from Tarsus in Cilicia, which was not an insignificant city.

Tarsus was incorporated into the Roman Empire in 67 BC, by the general Pompey and became the capital of the Roman province of Cilicia. It was here that Queen Cleopatra of Egypt and the Roman general and aristocrat Mark Antony first met. In the Roman period, the city was also an important intellectual centre, boasting its own academy. One of its leading disciples, the philosopher Athenodorus Cananites was the tutor of the first Roman emperor, Augustus, a fact which secured continuous imperial patronage for the city. When the province of Cilicia was divided, Tarsus remained the civil and religious metropolis of Cilicia Prima and was a grand city with palaces, marketplaces, roads and bridges, baths, fountains and waterworks, along with a gymnasium on the banks of the River Cyndus and a stadium.

Tarsus was the centre of Stoic philosophy. After Saul's conversion and his name change to Paul, he drew from his knowledge of Stoic philosophy, occasionally using Stoic terms and metaphors to assist

CHAPTER II

his new Gentile converts in their understanding of the revelation of God. In his sermon to the Greek audience in Athens recorded in Acts 17, he quoted from a number of Greek philosophers and poets.

Just how much Paul was influenced by Stoicism, if at all, is difficult to say and cannot be a matter of accurate knowledge. Paul, so far as is known, made no "acknowledgments" to Stoicism or any other Greek philosophical approach, if he had any to make; nor did he favour any philosophy with a criticism of its beliefs. As far as we know, the Stoics never recognise Paul, except to boo him out of the Areopagus in Athens when he attempted to address them, lauding him with the derogatory epithet, "Seed-gatherer!". The slang phrase was applied to men of small learning who, though not pupils of any of the philosophic teachers, had gained a scattering knowledge of philosophic terms, "pickers-up of learning's crumbs" and went about quoting their doctrines.

In his letters, some scholars have found references to his knowledge of Stoic ideas. Paul often used expressions and language that can be found in the writings of Seneca, Plato and Socrates. Though Paul may have read Stoic ideas and had knowledge of them, they were not the bedrock of his teaching and thinking.

Saul's birth in Tarsus enabled him to also claim Roman citizenship, and he acknowledged that his father was a citizen as well. For the first few centuries of the Christian era, Roman citizenship was a highly coveted prize, and Saul was apparently proud of his status as a Roman citizen.

When he was arrested for apparently causing a riot in the temple in Jerusalem, the garrison commander had Paul taken to the barracks and ordered Paul to be flogged and interrogated to find out why the people were shouting at and accusing him. As he was being stretched out for the flogging, Paul asked the centurion standing there if it was legal to flog a Roman citizen who hasn't even been found guilty. Upon hearing this, the centurion went to the commander and reported this new information about Paul's claim to be a Roman citizen. An interesting exchange followed between Paul and the commander which throws a lot of light on the value placed on Roman citizenship.

> *The commander went to Paul and asked, "Tell me, are you a Roman citizen?"*
> *"Yes, I am," Paul answered.*
> *Then the commander said, "I had to pay a lot of money for my citizenship."*
> *"But I was born a citizen," Paul retorted.*
> *Those who were about to interrogate and whip him withdrew immediately. The commander himself was alarmed when he realised he had put Paul, a Roman citizen, in chains (Acts 22:23-29).*

People could become a Roman citizen by birth or buying the privilege. Due to Rome's designation of Tarsus as a "free city", Paul's birth into a Jewish family within the Roman province of Cilicia in the city Tarsus granted him citizenship. The commander, however, had to pay a large sum of money to earn his right to citizenship.

Whilst having been born in Tarsus, Paul says that he was brought up in Jerusalem. In the first century, Jerusalem was an impressive city. It had a population of tens of thousands, by some estimates, even 100,000 or more. It was an ancient city dating back to the time of King David who had made it his capital. His son, King Solomon built the first temple in mid-10th century BC upon the Temple Mount also known as Mount Moriah, a hill in Jerusalem believed to be "the place that the Lord will choose" as his dwelling according to Deuteronomy 12:14-15. The city and the temple had

CHAPTER II

been destroyed by the Babylonians in the 586 BC. About half a century later, in 538 BC, Cyrus the Great, King of the Medes and the Persians, who had conquered the Babylonians, decreed that the Jewish exiles could return to Jerusalem and rebuild their temple.

With the encouragement of the prophets Haggai and Zechariah, Zerubbabel began construction of the second temple around 521 BC. The second temple was completed around 515 BC. It was then substantially enlarged by the dynasty established by Simon Maccabaeus that ruled Israel independently from 140-37 BC. At the end of the first century BC, the temple was completely refurbished and enlarged by Herod the Great. This temple was the most sacred site in the world for Jews and the only place where biblical tradition allowed animals to be sacrificed. This was the temple featured in the New Testament which Jesus regularly visited and Paul would have known.

In the late 50's AD, Paul still had family members living in the city, his sister's son being one of them. It was this boy who who took news of the plot to kill Paul to the garrison commander.

Paul said that while in Jerusalem he sat at the feet of Gamaliel and was taught "according to the perfect manner of the law of the fathers" (Acts 22:3). No details are given about which teachings Paul adopted from Gamaliel, as it is assumed that as a Pharisee, Paul was already recognised in the community at that time as a devout Jew.

The Acts of the Apostles introduces Gamaliel as a Pharisee and celebrated doctor of the Law of Moses. How much Gamaliel influenced aspects of Christianity is unmentioned other than this record of him presenting an argument against killing the apostles in Acts 5.

> "And now in the present case I advise you: Leave these men alone! Let them go! For if their purpose or activity is of

human origin, it will fail. But if it is from God, you will not be able to stop these men; you will only find yourselves fighting against God" (Acts 5:38-39).

The Talmud does describe Gamaliel as teaching a student who displayed "impudence in learning", which a few scholars identify as a possible reference to Paul. Helmut Koester, Professor of Divinity and of Ecclesiastical History at Harvard, questions if Paul studied under this famous rabbi, arguing that there is a marked contrast in the tolerance that Gamaliel is said to have expressed about Christianity with the "murderous rage" against Followers of the Way that Paul is described as having prior to his conversion in Acts 9:1.

What emerges is that Paul was clearly a Pharisee. He described himself as a Pharisee and the son of a Pharisee.

The word Pharisee is derived from an Aramaic word meaning, "separated." They were a group within Judaism that believed in the immortality of the soul, the resurrection of the dead, and punishment in future life for sin based upon how one behaved in this life. The souls of the wicked would be in prison forever under the earth, and those who were righteous would live again. This righteousness was related to obedience to Mosaic law. Where the Law was unspecific, they defined it in minute detail.

In Jesus' day, the Pharisees practiced their version of righteousness externally and very publicly. They were apparently more concerned with outward appearance than inward feeling. The Pharisees also added an enormous amount of traditional material that was passed down from one generation to the next.

They were at odds with the Sadducees and the Herodians, however, they all joined together against their common enemy, Jesus. The Pharisees were Jesus' chief persecutors. We find them being met with stern words from John where he was baptizing at

CHAPTER II

the Jordan river. "You brood of vipers! Who warned you to flee from the coming wrath?" (Matt. 3:7) The Pharisees accused Jesus of demonic practices and plotted his death for breaking the Sabbath. Jesus' strongest words of condemnation were aimed at the Pharisees.

"Woe to you, teachers of the law and Pharisees, you hypocrites! You shut the door of the kingdom of heaven in people's faces. You yourselves do not enter, nor will you let those enter who are trying to" (Matthew 23:13).

What led the Pharisees to interpret he Old Testament laws in such a legalistic and hypocritical way? The answer is found at the beginnings of men and the dawn of our relationship with God. I am greatly indebted to James Jordan for his understanding of these issues and the truth he has received and teaches in his book, *The Ancient Road Rediscovered*, where he explores these themes.

After the creation of the man, he is placed in a garden where two trees are described as growing. One is the Tree of Life whose fruit is life-giving and a source of untold blessing. The other is called the Tree of the Knowledge of Good and Evil. The man is told not to eat its fruit because when he does he will die. It is the tree that Satan used to tempt the man and the woman (ref. Genesis chapters 1-3).

The twenty-eighth chapter of the book of Ezekiel includes a prophetic picture that gives great insight into the origins of Satan and his behaviour. Though the prophetic utterance had immediate relevance to the King of Tyre, like much prophecy, it contained other truth. Traditionally, the Rabbis and Christian teachers have recognised the truths in the passage are related to the fall of Satan who is described as a created angelic being.

"You were the seal of perfection, full of wisdom and perfect in beauty. You were in Eden, the garden of God; You were anointed as a guardian cherub, for so I ordained you"

(Ezekiel 28:13-14,15)

Satan was a beautiful creature and very attractive. He is not the grotesque red creature with a tail and horns of popular imagination that owes its origins to Dante's *Inferno*.

Ezekiel 28:17 reveals exactly what happened to this creature.

"Your heart became proud on account of your beauty, and you corrupted your wisdom because of your splendour."

According to a similar passage in Isaiah 14, Satan was corrupted because of his desire to replace God with himself. Satan's wisdom is a corrupted wisdom. In the temptation of the man and the woman recorded in Genesis 3:4-5, Satan applied his corrupted wisdom.

"You will not certainly die," the serpent said to the woman. "For God knows that when you eat from it your eyes will be opened, and you will be like God, knowing good and evil."

Satan draws them in with the desire to eat.

"When the woman saw that the fruit of the tree was good for food and pleasing to the eye, and also desirable for gaining wisdom, she took some and ate it. She also gave some to her husband, who was with her, and he ate it. Then the eyes of both of them were opened, and they realised they were naked; so they sewed fig leaves together and made coverings for themselves" (Genesis 3:6-7).

The eyes of both of them were opened but not their physical eyes because they could see already. The question is what eyes were opened? It was their capacity to see good and evil. They had eaten from the Tree of the Knowledge of Good and Evil. The tree is Satan's tree that would lead them into his perspective. From then on mankind's understanding would originate in Satan's warped perspective of wanting to be like God, "I will make myself like the most high" (Isa 14:14). This is still seen in contemporary Christian thinking where the fulfilment of the Christian life is seen to be achieving something for God, doing something for God or serving God. God's perspective is that we walk with him, be with him and receive life from him.

Adam and his wife, immediately evaluated according to right and wrong. Their nakedness felt bad, and their thought process was, "This is bad we have to fix the wrong with the good."

This has been the problem for all humanity ever since. We recognise the bad we have done and try to replace it by doing good, rationalizing this as our relationship with God. Fallen man's way of relating to God becomes the trap of evaluating everything as either right or wrong. As soon as we do the right thing to counterbalance the wrong, the list of what we must do in order to be right just gets longer and longer.

Satan's wisdom is appealing. It is very hard to argue against someone who displays what is absolutely right. However, it is a corrupted wisdom. It becomes a cultural thing, to do the right thing and get it right. And woe betide anyone who gets it wrong. There is little or no mercy in this mind set.

The problem with the tree is that it looks good and it becomes a self-righteous issue. The whole human race has been walking according to this satanic wisdom ever since. Wrong tree wisdom! Judgment of those who do not behave according to received wisdom is quickly meted out. Holiness is confused with righteousness. Holy means other than, separate. God is "other than" anything in this world. The wrong tree thinking equates holiness with correct religious activity rather than being like God. Righteousness becomes an issue of good and bad, right and wrong, doing good and obeying God. We have turned these things into a behaviour issue.

By the time of the coming of Jesus, Judaism had established a culture within the sect of the Pharisees that was totally "wrong tree".

Paul's own testimony was that he was a Pharisee and had been brought up in Jerusalem. This raises the question of whether Paul as the young Saul of Tarsus in Jerusalem had ever heard Jesus speak or seen him in action. When Saul meets the risen Jesus on the Damascus road and is commissioned by him to be his witness, according to Paul's own words when on trial before King Agrippa, Jesus says, "I have appeared to you to appoint you as a servant and as a witness of what you have seen and will see of me" (Acts 25:16).

This suggests Paul may have seen Jesus before this encounter on the road to Damascus, but it is difficult to say if this is the case. In Paul's letters and his sermons recorded by Luke in Acts, there are very few suggestions that he had heard Jesus speak. However, there is evidence that he had knowledge of a number of the events surrounding Jesus' life and more particularly the ministry of John the Baptist.

Paul frequently mentioned the ministry of John the Baptist when addressing Jewish hearers in his early missionary travels. In Pisidian, Antioch, whilst preaching in the synagogue, Paul says,

> *"Before the coming of Jesus, John preached repentance and baptism to all the people of Israel. As John was completing his work, he said: 'Who do you suppose I am? I am not the one you are looking for. But there is one coming after me whose sandals I am not worthy to untie'"* (Acts 13:24-25).

This reference is very similar to the sayings of John recorded in the gospels.

Significantly in Matthew's Gospel we read,

> *"People went out to him from Jerusalem and all Judea and the whole region of the Jordan. Confessing their sins, they were baptised by him in the Jordan River. But when he*

CHAPTER II

saw many of the Pharisees and Sadducees coming to where he was baptising, he said to them: "You brood of vipers! Who warned you to flee from the coming wrath? Produce fruit in keeping with repentance. And do not think you can say to yourselves, 'We have Abraham as our father.' I tell you that out of these stones God can raise up children for Abraham" (Matthew 3:5-9).

It would not be inconceivable that the young Pharisee Saul of Tarsus may have been one of those who went out to hear John preach in the Jordan Valley and heard these words for himself.

The question whether Saul had ever heard or seen Jesus is more difficult. There are few quotations or even allusions to any of the teachings or words of Jesus in Paul's preaching or letters. The one time he does quote a saying of Jesus it is one that is not found in any of the gospels. When saying goodbye to the leaders of the church in Ephesus, he says,

"In everything I showed you that by working hard in this manner you must help the weak and remember the words of the Lord Jesus, that he himself said, 'It is more blessed to give than to receive'" (Acts 20:35).

The only other time Paul quotes the words of Jesus relates to the institution of the Lord's supper which clearly was an occasion where Paul could not have heard them spoken in their original context. They do, however, indicate the widespread use of these words by Christians from the earliest times when celebrating the Lord's Supper.

One aspect of the life of Jesus that the Pharisee Saul was absolutely convinced about was that Jesus had really died. In Paul's first major recorded sermon in Acts 13, some years before the gospels were written, Luke quotes Paul's account of the final days of Jesus life.

> "The people of Jerusalem and their rulers did not recognise Jesus, yet in condemning him they fulfilled the words of the prophets that are read every Sabbath. Though they found no proper ground for a death sentence, they asked Pilate to have him executed. When they had carried out all that was written about him, they took him down from the cross and laid him in a tomb. But God raised him from the dead, and for many days he was seen by those who had traveled with him from Galilee to Jerusalem. They are now his witnesses to our people" (Acts 13:27-31).

Where Paul has knowledge of events, he is quite specific. One example is in the list of resurrection appearance by Jesus that Paul records in his first letter to the Corinthians.

> "...he appeared to Cephas, and then to the Twelve. After that, he appeared to more than five hundred of the brothers and sisters at the same time, most of whom are still living, though some have fallen asleep. Then he appeared to James, then to all the apostles, and last of all he appeared to me also, as to one abnormally born" (1 Corinthians 15:5-8).

Saul of Tarsus makes his first appearance at the events surrounding the stoning of Stephen who was one of the leaders of the early church in Jerusalem. As recorded in the Acts of the Apostles, "Meanwhile, the witnesses laid their coats at the feet of a young man named Saul. And Saul approved of their killing him" (Acts 7:58).

Luke continues,

> "On that day a great persecution broke out against the church in Jerusalem, and all except the apostles were scattered throughout Judea and Samaria. Godly men buried Stephen and mourned deeply for him. But Saul began to destroy the church. Going from house to house,

CHAPTER II

he dragged off both men and women and put them in prison" (Acts 8:1-2).

Then in Acts 9, Luke wrote that Saul was still breathing out murderous threats against the Lord's disciples. He went to the high priest and asked him for letters to the synagogues in Damascus, so that if he found any there who belonged to the Way, whether men or women, he might take them as prisoners to Jerusalem.

In Paul's own words when on trial in front of King Agrippa and Queen Bernice, he described his actions and motivation for his behaviour in those days.

"I too was convinced that I ought to do all that was possible to oppose the name of Jesus of Nazareth. And that is just what I did in Jerusalem. On the authority of the chief priests I put many of the Lord's people in prison, and when they were put to death, I cast my vote against them. Many a time I went from one synagogue to another to have them punished, and I tried to force them to blaspheme. I was so obsessed with persecuting them that I even hunted them down in foreign cities. On one of these journeys I went to Damascus with the authority and commission of the chief priests" (Acts 26:9-12).

The honesty and frankness of Paul's description of his actions is shocking. His use of the word obsessive gives a strong impression of his mental attitude during that time. His obsessive persecution of the early church began with approval of Stephen's stoning and was quickly followed by leading a sustained attack on the wider church. People were hunted down and arrested in Jerusalem and thrown into prison where Paul assented to their executions. Paul admits that he personally had Followers of the Way punished and tried to force them to deny Christ and renounce their faith.

The level of persecution gives credence to how deeply committed the new converts were to their new-found faith and how resistant they were to being coerced into changing and going back to their former lives within Judaism. Willing to resist even to the point of martyrdom, they were the first of many hundreds of thousands in centuries to come who would walk the path of martyrdom to their own Golgotha. Two hundred years later, a North African Christian writer named Tertullian wrote, "the blood of the martyrs is the seed of the Church" (*Apologeticus*, Chapter 50). Persecution has always resulted in the opposite effect for the Church. Through the centuries, non-Christians observing the courage and fortitude of Christian martyrs have been converted themselves.

Recently, a Ugandan friend shared how he as a young Muslim boy converted to Christianity during the persecution of Christians by the regime of the dictator Idi Amin in the 1970s in Uganda. Christians and Muslims had lived peacefully alongside each other for years in his village, until one day Amin's security forces entered the village and commanded all the Christians to gather on the main street. Once assembled, they were all brutally slaughtered in front of their Muslim neighbours. This deeply traumatised him. He reported that it was their courage and the way they embraced their deaths without fear that convinced him of the reality of their beliefs. Soon after, he became a Christian. This man is now a leader in the church in Uganda with a clear revelation of the truth about Jesus and God as Father.

The persecution that Saul instigated and personally participated in was indicative of a deeply troubled personality. On one occasion, I talked to a psychiatrist about this passage, and he commented that someone who exhibited such behaviour would have been very disturbed and probably psychopathic!

CHAPTER II

Saul's behaviour before his conversion was very revealing. He was a well-known Pharisee and very strict as far as the keeping of the law was concerned. The Pharisees were a powerful enough group in Jewish society to demand the death penalty for those they judged as being law breakers. Saul would have perceived God as stern and concerned with correct behaviour rather than relationship. His understanding of the nature of Jewish religion was that of a lawyer or a typical legalistic Pharisee.

To Saul the Pharisee, this strict adherence to the Law would have required a tremendous exercise of the will. Meticulous keeping of perceived rules by the sheer act of the will without empathy for others is another trait that has been observed in a psychopathic character. He would have felt driven or compelled to exercise his will in this way and perceived it as obedience to the law. This meant that he imprisoned people, had people whipped for believing in Jesus, and tortured them while overseeing their deaths. This adherence to the Law led him to persecute others in a cold, heartless manner as a determined act of the will with impunity and without apparent concern for the feelings of those he was persecuting.

Saul of Tarsus, the Pharisee brought up in Jerusalem, the persecutor of the early church said in his own words before his own people in the temple in Jerusalem,

> *"I am a Jew, born in Tarsus of Cilicia, but brought up in this city. I studied under Gamaliel and was thoroughly trained in the law of our ancestors. I was just as zealous for God as any of you are today. I persecuted the followers of this Way to their death, arresting both men and women and throwing them into prison, as the high priest and all the Council can themselves testify. I even obtained letters from them to their associates in Damascus and went*

there to bring these people as prisoners to Jerusalem to be punished (Acts 22:3-4).

In Acts 26, he talks about the journey to Damascus as one among many, except on this day everything would change for Saul of Tarsus.

CHAPTER III

THE ENCOUNTER ON THE ROAD TO DAMASCUS.

Their journey began in Jerusalem, and they had taken the road down towards Jericho which drops right into the Jordan Valley. Once there, Saul made enquires of the whereabouts of one man he was particularly interested in arresting. A former tax collector called Zacchaeus who had embraced this nonsense about Jesus. The locals reported that he had fled to the coast and might be in Caesarea. Zacchaeus would have to wait. Damascus was the destination for now.

They turned north and took the road alongside the River Jordan. As they passed through, Saul remembered how all this began when John the Baptist started his preaching in this area. Preaching about righteousness and dealing with sin was one thing, but then it shifted to the newcomer Jesus and it all blew up. The authorities thought it was dealt with when John was beheaded by Herod and Jesus was later crucified. At least no one said John had risen from the dead. Saul knew Jesus was dead beyond any shadow of a doubt. He saw what crucifixion did to people; he knew all about the cross. Jesus was dead, it was impossible for him to be alive. After all, if he was indeed risen that would change everything and he couldn't think about that. Something was niggling inside of him all the time which he pushed to the back of his mind. He could not allow himself to think about this bizarre possibility.

THE ENCOUNTER ON THE ROAD TO DAMASCUS

The road wound up the hills through the east of Lake Galilee and into the foothills of Mt Hermon. Soon, they were in the province of Syria technically outside any Jewish jurisdiction. They would need to be careful whom they spoke to until they reached Damascus and connected with the local Jewish leaders there. It was getting hotter and hotter each day. They were nearly there, just one more day.

It had been his plan to avoid travelling in the heat of the day, but they would find it hard to get to the city and reach the safety of its walls before sunset. It was the tenth day of walking, with only one day of rest, the Sabbath of course. Driven by his desire to get to Damascus and round up some of the ring leaders of the pernicious sect known as Followers of the Way, Saul had pushed his small group of men to march as fast as they could. Now they were nearing the end of their long trek from Jerusalem to Damascus, and he would bound these dissidents and bring them back to Jerusalem where he would interrogate them using his special techniques. Many of them refused to deny their allegiance, and he was haunted by their courage and resolve to willingly face execution. They had said they felt it a privilege to be witnesses for their misguided belief in this Jesus.

He loathed the very mention of the name of Jesus of Nazareth. Everyone was talking about him. In the many of the towns and villages they had passed through, people pointed and whispered when they recognised the great persecutor as some called him. He could hear them mentioning that wretched Nazarene's name.

The morning heat was blistering, the road hot and dusty. Saul's eyes, prone to infection, were sore and inflamed from dust and sweat, rubbing only made them worse. They decided to stop, eat some bread, have a drink of the rancid wine they carried and rest in any shade they could find. There was very little in this sun-bleached landscape. It was approaching noon as Saul looked around for somewhere to rest, and

CHAPTER III

suddenly, a light brighter than the midday sun blazed around him. Saul could not see anything. He staggered and fell to the ground. His eyes hurt and he could not see. Then he heard a voice. "Saul, Saul, why are you persecuting me?"

∿∧⋁∧∿

A 'Damascus Road experience' has become a figure of speech used widely in literature and understood as a radical transformation or conversion. That certainly was the case for Saul of Tarsus whose experience gives us this phrase.

Saul was on his way to Damascus to continue his persecution of the early church. The early church was not referred to as Christians at this time, instead they were known as Followers of the Way.

What do we know about them and their beginnings? Whilst it may not have been the earliest document written, the Acts of the Apostles describe the events of the beginnings of the church. Acts begins with what happened after Jesus was crucified and raised from the dead. Luke, later a travelling companion of Paul, wrote Acts. It is of course Luke's second volume following on from his Gospel. Like the Gospels, in the Acts of the Apostles, we have many eyewitness accounts of the events the book describes.

Luke himself was present at some of the events that are described in the latter part of the book and was therefore an eyewitness of what he writes about. The Gospels may not have been written until 60AD at the earliest, so Luke's account of Acts gives us invaluable information of how the early church began and developed even though he wrote it after he had written his gospel.

The Acts of the Apostles describes the beginnings of the church in Jerusalem that was essentially a Jewish church. In Acts chapters

1 through 7, the activity took place in and around Jerusalem. Then the church began to touch the Gentile world in Acts chapters 8 through 12 as the apostles encountered Gentiles such as Cornelius the Roman centurion and the Ethiopian eunuch. The church also began to face persecution and later, James the son of Zebedee, Jesus' cousin, was the first of the apostles to be martyred.

The Followers of the Way were mostly Jewish converts and followers of Jesus. In the upper room on the last night he was with his disciples, Jesus described himself, amongst other things, as 'the Way'. These Jewish followers were people from the immediate vicinity of Jerusalem and surrounding areas, including Galilee. Luke reports that many Jews from far away cities and provinces that made up the Roman empire who had been in Jerusalem for the Feast of Pentecost had joined the band of followers of Jesus. The list Luke provides shows the extraordinary spread of the Jewish Diaspora at that time. These were Jews who described themselves as:

"Parthians, Medes and Elamites; residents of Mesopotamia, Judea and Cappadocia, Pontus and Asia, Phrygia and Pamphylia, Egypt and the parts of Libya near Cyrene; visitors from Rome, both Jews and converts to Judaism; Cretans and Arabs, we hear them declaring the wonders of God in our own tongues" (Acts 2: 9-11).

Luke wrote about thousands responding to the preaching of the leaders of the church. Three thousand alone were baptised on the Day of Pentecost following Simon Peter's sermon in Acts 2:41. After the remarkable healing of a lame man at the Temple gate by Peter and John and their subsequent arrest, many more responded and became followers.

"But many who heard the message believed; so the number of men who believed grew to about five thousand" (Acts 4:4).

CHAPTER III

We get some idea of the community life of these early Followers of the Way in this passage from Acts 4.

> *"All the believers were one in heart and mind. No one claimed that any of their possessions was their own, but they shared everything they had. With great power the apostles continued to testify to the resurrection of the Lord Jesus. And God's grace was so powerfully at work in them all that there were no needy persons among them. For from time to time those who owned land or houses sold them, brought the money from the sales and put it at the apostles' feet, and it was distributed to anyone who had need. Joseph, a Levite from Cyprus, whom the apostles called Barnabas (which means "son of encouragement"), sold a field he owned and brought the money and put it at the apostles' feet" (Acts 4:32-37).*

Luke continues,

> *"The apostles performed many signs and wonders among the people. And all the believers used to meet together in Solomon's Colonnade. No one else dared join them, even though they were highly regarded by the people. Nevertheless, more and more men and women believed in the Lord and were added to their number. As a result, people brought the sick into the streets and laid them on beds and mats so that at least Peter's shadow might fall on some of them as he passed by. Crowds gathered also from the towns around Jerusalem, bringing their sick and those tormented by impure spirits, and all of them were healed" (Acts 5:12-16).*

> *"Day after day, in the temple courts and from house to house, they never stopped teaching and proclaiming the*

> good news that Jesus is the Messiah" (Acts 5:41).
>
> "In those days when the number of disciples was increasing, the Greek speaking Jews among them complained against the Hebrew speaking Jews because their widows were being overlooked in the daily distribution of food. So the Twelve gathered all the disciples together and said, "It would not be right for us to neglect the ministry of the word of God in order to wait on tables. Brothers and sisters, choose seven men from among you who are known to be full of the Spirit and wisdom. We will turn this responsibility over to them and will give our attention to prayer and the ministry of the word." This proposal pleased the whole group. They chose Stephen, a man full of faith and of the Holy Spirit; also Philip, Procorus, Nicanor, Timon, Parmenas, and Nicolas from Antioch, a convert to Judaism. They presented these men to the apostles, who prayed and laid their hands on them. So the word of God spread. The number of disciples in Jerusalem increased rapidly, and a large number of priests became obedient to the faith" (Acts 6:1-6).

This last comment by Luke is interesting because it revealed that members of the priestly class in Jerusalem had become Followers of the Way. Acts 15:5 says that some of the believers also belonged to the party of the Pharisees. None are named, but there are references in the Gospels that specifically refer to a number of Pharisees by name who were sympathetic to the teaching of Jesus and the early church. Gamaliel has been mentioned already when he urged the Sanhedrin to wait and not rush into condemning the new group.

Nicodemus, a prominent Jerusalem Pharisee, had visited and talked with Jesus under the cover of darkness in John 3. In John

CHAPTER III

7, Nicodemus advised his colleagues among "the chief priests and the Pharisees", to hear and investigate before making a judgment concerning Jesus. Their mocking response to Nicodemus argued that no prophet ever came from Galilee. Nonetheless, it is probable that he wielded a certain influence in the Sanhedrin. When Jesus was to be buried, he and Joseph of Arimathea petitioned the Roman Governor Pontius Pilate for permission to bury Jesus' body, and Joseph provided his own tomb for the purpose.

Joseph of Arimathea is mentioned in all four Gospels. Matthew 27:57 described him simply as a rich man and a disciple of Jesus, but according to Mark 15:43, Joseph of Arimathea was a respected member of the council who was also himself looking for the kingdom of God. While Luke 23:50-56 adds that he had not consented to the council's action.

According to John 19:38, upon hearing of Jesus' death, this secret follower of Jesus asked Pilate if he could take away the body of Jesus, and Pilate granted him permission. Joseph immediately purchased a linen shroud and proceeded to the crucifixion site to take the body of Jesus down from the cross. Then, according to John 19:39 - 40, Joseph and Nicodemus took the body and bound it in linen cloths with the spices Nicodemus bought. Nicodemus had purchased about 100 Roman pounds or 33 kilograms of myrrh and aloe for the purpose of embalming Jesus' body according to Jewish custom. The disciples then conveyed the prepared corpse to a man-made cave hewn from rock in a garden of Joseph's house nearby. The Gospel of Matthew alone suggests that this was Joseph's own tomb. The burial was undertaken speedily because of the rapid onset of the Sabbath.

Luke, in the seventh chapter of his Gospel, also reports that Jesus had dinner with a Galilean Pharisee who is mentioned by name as Simon. The detail in Luke's story includes the inner thoughts of

THE ENCOUNTER ON THE ROAD TO DAMASCUS

this Pharisee which suggests he personally related the story to Luke and as a result allowed his name to be mentioned.

Whether any of these three Pharisees were also Followers of the Way is impossible to conclude from the biblical record, however the traditions of the church from very early days has accorded them the status of sainthood and named saints days after them.

For the Followers of the Way, the primary issue that identified them as a group was that they believed Jesus was the promised Messiah, the anointed Son of God who had been unjustly arrested, tried and crucified. However, after he was declared dead and buried, he was miraculously raised from the dead on the day following the Jewish sabbath. He then appeared alive to a large number of people over many days who confirmed his resurrection before he was taken up in a cloud, returning to his Father in heaven.

Some of their earliest statements clearly describe what they believed. On the day of Pentecost soon after the Holy Spirit had fallen on the one hundred and twenty that were gathered together, Peter stood to explain what had happened and announced,

> "Jesus of Nazareth was a man accredited by God to you by miracles, wonders and signs, which God did among you through him, as you yourselves know. This man was handed over to you by God's deliberate plan and foreknowledge; and you, with the help of wicked men, put him to death by nailing him to the cross. But God raised him from the dead, freeing him from the agony of death, because it was impossible for death to keep its hold on him" (Acts 2:20-24).

A few days later, following the healing of a lame man, this explanation was given,

> "It is by the name of Jesus Christ of Nazareth, whom you

CHAPTER III

crucified but whom God raised from the dead, that this man stands before you healed" (Acts 4:10).

It was against this back story that Saul of Tarsus, a Pharisee, resident in Jerusalem was driven to begin his murderous persecution of the Followers of the Way.

The persecution that erupted as Saul set out for Damascus was severe and brutal. In Acts 9, Luke presented his short, succinct version of the events.

> *"As he neared Damascus on his journey, suddenly a light from heaven flashed around him. He fell to the ground and heard a voice say to him, "Saul, Saul, why do you persecute me?"*
>
> *"Who are you, Lord?" Saul asked.*
>
> *"I am Jesus, whom you are persecuting," he replied. "Now get up and go into the city, and you will be told what you must do."*

The men traveling with Saul stood there speechless; they heard the sound but did not see anyone. Saul got up from the ground, but when he opened his eyes he could see nothing, so they led him by the hand into Damascus. For three days he was blind and did not eat or drink anything.

The second telling of Saul's conversion occurs in a speech he gave when arrested in Jerusalem in Acts 22. Paul, as he is known by then, addressed the crowd and told them of his conversion with essentially the same description as Acts 9, but with slight differences.

For example, Acts 9:7 notes that Saul's companions did not see who he was speaking to while Acts 22:9 indicates they did share in seeing the light. This speech was most likely originally given in Aramaic, with the Acts 22 passage being a Greek translation and summary. The speech was clearly tailored for its Jewish audience

THE ENCOUNTER ON THE ROAD TO DAMASCUS

with stress placed upon Ananias's good reputation among Jews in Damascus rather than his Christianity.

Though briefer than the others, the final account of Saul's conversion was delivered in front of Agrippa, Berenice and Festus which Luke records in Acts 26. The speech, again tailored for its audience, emphasised what a Roman ruler would understand: the need to obey a heavenly vision and reassuring Agrippa that Christians were not a secret society.

Saul's own words add extra detail to the event such as, it happened at noon. Saul also comments that Jesus spoke to him in the Hebrew dialect which the NIV translates as Aramaic. Aramaic would have been the native language Jesus spoke growing up in Galilee as well as the language most people spoke in the Roman Province of Judea. It was quite possibly Saul's native tongue as well. The fact that Jesus spoke to Saul in his mother tongue suggests a degree of intimacy that would have surprised him.

In all accounts, it is related that Saul's name is repeated twice by the risen Jesus. "Saul, Saul, why are you persecuting me?" Without realizing that repeating a person's name is a Hebrew expression of intimacy, it would be easy to miss the strength of this statement. When Jesus confronted Martha after her performance driven, over the top dinner arrangements, instead of scolding her, he said, "Martha, Martha". When Jesus warned Peter about his denials that were about to happen, Jesus lovingly said, "Peter, Peter." When Jesus wept over Jerusalem, he addressed the city as, "Oh Jerusalem, Jerusalem". In each case, we find the word repeated for intimacy's sake. In spite of all Saul had done against Jesus and his followers, he is still addressed with intimacy and affection.

Saul added that after Jesus asked why was Saul persecuting him, Jesus continued with, "It is hard for you to kick against the goads".

CHAPTER III

The saying is a Greek proverb related to the goad used by farmers to 'encourage' an ox to go in the right direction when ploughing and implied that in the preceding months, perhaps years, Saul's conscience may have troubled or pricked him, but Jesus seems to be the author of these challenges. Evidently, Jesus had been trying to get Saul's attention for quite some time. Perhaps the impact of the numerous deaths he witnessed and courage of people who refused to deny their faith in Jesus had not left him untouched or unmoved.

It would have been a great challenge for Saul to realise the one speaking directly to him was the one he had persecuted, insisted was dead and buried and whom, in his opinion, had certainly not risen from the dead.

Saul asked, "Who are you, Lord?"

"I am Jesus, whom you are persecuting," the Lord replied.

It is not difficult to imagine the stunning impact these words had on Saul.

It was an encounter that marked the beginning of his complete transformation. As a Pharisee, he had believed in the possibility of resurrection. On the road to Damascus he experienced it first-hand as he encountered the risen Christ. This was the beginning of a completely new way of seeing everything for Saul of Tarsus. As a Pharisee, he had been driven by his immense intellectual ability. On this day, he was having an experience that challenged everything his mind, reason, and intellect had thought. Everything he had believed up to this point in his life was about to change. From this encounter forward, Saul would experience and see things with the eyes of his heart rather than his intellect. Then having seen and experienced things, he would use his great gift of teaching to define and explain those things so others would see and experience also. Changed by

THE ENCOUNTER ON THE ROAD TO DAMASCUS

an experience at the heart level, his mind would become renewed.

The approach of many Christians for centuries has been to put the cart before the horse. We have believed that conversion or becoming a Christian was an intellectual exercise of the changing of our minds rather than an experience or an encounter with the risen Christ. In post Reformation and Evangelical teaching, there has been a recognition of this life changing encounter with Jesus, but this is quickly subsumed into intellectual transformation. There has almost been a fear of experience and a belief that the only real proof of genuine conversion is when the mind is transformed and renewed. Indeed, it is Paul's own words in Romans 12:2 that we are to be transformed by the renewing of the mind that is often quoted and held up as a pattern. The simple fact is transformation of the mind takes place after encounter and experience happens in the heart. Romans 12 follows eleven chapters that describe this heart-based experience.

For Saul, this encounter was nothing less than a personal appearance to him of the resurrected Jesus. When writing in First Corinthians 15 about the resurrection of Jesus he says,

> *"For what I received I passed on to you as of first importance: that Christ died for our sins according to the Scriptures, that he was buried, that he was raised on the third day according to the Scriptures, and that he appeared to Cephas, and then to the Twelve. After that, he appeared to more than five hundred of the brothers and sisters at the same time, most of whom are still living, though some have fallen asleep. Then he appeared to James, then to all the apostles, and last of all he appeared to me also, as to one abnormally born. For I am the least of the apostles and do not even deserve to be called an apostle, because*

CHAPTER III

I persecuted the church of God" (1 Corinthians 15:3-8).

For Saul, this was the great turning point, the great encounter that he considered as foundational and of utmost importance. Becoming a Follower of the Way meant a foundational belief in the death of Jesus for our sins, his burial and his resurrection on the third day. In 1 Corinthians, he wrote these things in a way that later generations would include in the great creedal statements of the Church. He then appealed to the resurrection appearances as proof of the truth of these statements. By the time he wrote 1 Corinthians, he had met with Peter and others of the leaders of the Church and heard about their own encounters with the resurrected Jesus. He mentioned a number of appearances not recorded in the Gospels. This included a personal appearance to Cephas, that is Peter and also to James, the brother of Jesus. Then also an appearance to a large group of over five hundred men and women many of whom were still living at the time of his writing. Lastly, he related his own experience of the resurrected Jesus on the road to Damascus among these resurrection appearances.

The story continued in his own account in Acts 26 where he added significant new details. What follows is a full and detailed account by Saul of his call to ministry that he received from Jesus.

> *"Now get up and stand on your feet. I have appeared to you to appoint you as a servant and as a witness of what you have seen and will see of me. I will rescue you from your own people and from the Gentiles. I am sending you to them to open their eyes and turn them from darkness to light, and from the power of Satan to God, so that they may receive forgiveness of sins and a place among those who are sanctified by faith in me" (Acts 26:16-18).*

The rest of Saul's life was defined by this moment. Whenever he

THE ENCOUNTER ON THE ROAD TO DAMASCUS

looked back on his life, this moment and the call he experienced on the Damascus road was the defining moment of transformation, specifically recounting that Jesus appeared to him personally in order to convince him that he was alive and appoint him for a specific task in a specific role.

"I have appeared to you to appoint you as a servant and as a witness..."

It began with an appointment, or a setting apart for a specific purpose, function and ministry. Jesus appointed Saul for this purpose and used two words that would be the hallmark of his ministry, a servant and a witness. Both words are loaded with significance. Together, they coalesced into a distinctly new word that the Early Church would coin to describe those who had been gifted and set apart as a foundational ministry. This is the word "apostle".

From the very beginning of this appointment by Jesus, the heart of Saul's ministry is revealed. It is a description of apostolic ministry that is characterised by servanthood and bearing witness. The Greek words are significant as the first is 'huperetes' which is literally an under-oarsman, one of the lowest ranks of rowers in a Roman galley. It is that of a subordinate or assistant who is acting under another's direction. It can be translated servant but there is a depth to the word that does not indicate status or title rather one who is dependant on a superior for leadership direction and instruction. Jesus was first and foremost calling Saul to be a man under his direct authority. To act under his direction and leadership. Paul uses the word in his first letter to the Corinthians to describe his role in relation to Jesus.

"This, then, is how you ought to regard us: as servants of Christ" (1 Corinthians 4:1).

When writing most of his letters in the New Testament, Paul picked up this sense of his calling and designation by Jesus to be an

CHAPTER III

apostle and used the term to describe his calling and appointment coming directly by Jesus and God the Father.

"Paul, called to be an apostle of Christ Jesus by the will of God" (1 Corinthians. 1:1; 2 Corinthians 1:1).

"Paul, an apostle—sent not from men nor by a man, but by Jesus Christ and God the Father, who raised him from the dead" (Galatians 1:1).

"Paul, an apostle of Christ Jesus by the will of God" (Ephesians 1:1; Colossians 1:1).

"Paul, an apostle of Christ Jesus by the command of God our Saviour and of Christ Jesus our hope" (1 Timothy 1:1).

"Paul, an apostle of Christ Jesus by the will of God, in keeping with the promise of life that is in Christ Jesus" (2 Timothy 1:1).

In the New Testament a number of other individuals are described as apostles including Barnabas. In Romans 16:7 Andronicus and Junia, relatives of Paul are described as being notable among the apostles and they apparently were Christians before Paul.

After the death of the initial twelve apostles recognised in the New Testament, the word was no longer used to describe a function or a ministry but rather a historic title given to the first twelve apostles and Paul. From very early on in the Christian era, this word began to be seen as a title or an office rather than a description of a specific ministry function. Indeed, after the close of the New Testament era, no one is given this title within the Church. It is not until the twentieth century that the word re-emerged as a ministry and increasingly as a title.

Paul also used the word servant in the opening statement of Romans, Philippians and Titus. However, he chose another word to describe his servanthood in these letters, the word 'doulos'.

THE ENCOUNTER ON THE ROAD TO DAMASCUS

A similar word used to describe a bonded servant, literally a slave, this again is a strong word. It does not describe an employee as a servant might be, rather it is the household slave whose life is completely under the direction of his master.

> "Paul, a servant of Christ Jesus, called to be an apostle and set apart for the gospel of God" (Romans 1:1).
> "Paul and Timothy, servants of Christ Jesus" (Philippians 1:1).
> "Paul, a servant of God and an apostle of Jesus Christ" (Titus 1:1).

Paul took up this theme in his letter to the Philippians when describing the attitudes that servants of Jesus have.

> "In your relationships with one another, have the same mindset as Christ Jesus: Who, being in very nature God, did not consider equality with God something to be used to his own advantage; rather, he made himself nothing by taking the very nature of a servant" (Philippians 2:5-7).

We are encouraged by Paul to operate as servants in the same way as Jesus did. He was not seeking to hold on to his status as the eternal Son of God and willingly laid that down, and as a son secure in his identity, he had the heart of a servant or literally a bond slave. We will explore this theme of living as sons in relation to God as a Father in greater detail as this is a major revelation that Paul received from God.

The second word that Jesus used when addressing Saul is 'martura' which is the root word for martyr, translated here as a witness. A witness is a person who has seen something and bears testimony to what has been seen. In later centuries, the word was specifically linked to people who had been executed for their beliefs or rather martyred. A whole new group or class of people began to be

CHAPTER III

described as "the Martyrs".

When Jesus used the word to address Saul, he was talking about the function that Saul would have of bearing testimony to what he had personally witnessed.

What had Saul witnessed personally? What had he seen of Jesus prior to this?

Saul's obsessive persecution of the Followers of the Way was because they were just as convinced that Jesus was alive as he was that Jesus was dead. Saul's insistence on the fact that Jesus was not alive may have been because he had personally witnessed the crucifixion. There is no hard evidence of this in anything he specifically said or wrote, however, there is the fact that an explanation of what happened on the cross and its significance was very prominent in Paul's preaching and writing.

The 'preaching of the cross' was the distinctive message of the apostle Paul. It was the gospel he preached, that Christ died for our sins and rose from the dead for our salvation. No other New Testament writer has such clear and detailed understanding of the significance of the death of Jesus on the cross as Paul, coupled with that is an emphasis on the blood of Christ.

Jesus told Saul he wanted him to testify about what he had seen. Jesus also said he would show Saul things. In this statement, there is a clear indication that Jesus would reveal truth to Saul that others may not yet have seen or understood. Later he wrote to the church in Galatia,

> *"I want you to know, brothers and sisters, that the gospel I preached is not of human origin. I did not receive it from any man, nor was I taught it; rather, I received it by revelation from Jesus Christ" (Galatians 1:11-12).*

The implication was that throughout his life and ministry, Paul

THE ENCOUNTER ON THE ROAD TO DAMASCUS

would be on the receiving end of direct revelation from Jesus about the nature of all that God was doing in Christ.

Before we look at the nature of this revelation in more detail, we need to see what else Jesus said to Saul and what unfolded when he went to Damascus. Jesus, having appointed and commissioned him to be his servant and a witness to the things he had seen and would be shown, went on to reassure Saul that he would be with him and specifically that he would testify before the Gentiles. Jesus promised to rescue Saul from all those who would oppose him, both among his own people, the Jews, and also the non-Jewish Gentiles.

"I will rescue you from your own people and from the Gentiles. I am sending you to them to open their eyes and turn them from darkness to light, and from the power of Satan to God so that they may receive forgiveness of sins and a place among those who are sanctified by faith in me" (Acts 26:17-18).

Jesus told Saul what his ministry would fundamentally be about, saying that he was sending him to the Gentiles to open their eyes. Once their eyes were opened, the effect would turn them from darkness to light, from living under Satan's power to living under God's power. This would result in forgiveness of sins and a place where they could belong and live the holy and blameless life of faith. There are many threads and strands that become much clearer as Jesus showed Saul these things by revelation.

The key to all of this lies in the statement, "to open their eyes". This is a direct link back to the events that took place in the Garden of Eden in Genesis 3. I have already written about the Tree of the Knowledge of Good and Evil that was in the garden and how eating from the fruit of this wrong tree has led to incalculable damage to the human race. We have seen how the Pharisees had

CHAPTER III

been completely misled in their understanding of how mankind was to relate to God. In Genesis 3, Satan's temptation of Adam and his wife was about convincing them that they would be like God if they ate from this tree. Satan asked them,

> *Did God really say, "You must not eat from any tree in the garden?"*
>
> *The woman said to the serpent, "We may eat fruit from the trees in the garden, but God did say, 'You must not eat fruit from the tree that is in the middle of the garden, and you must not touch it, or you will die.'"*
>
> *"You will not certainly die," the serpent said to the woman. "For God knows that when you eat from it your eyes will be opened, and you will be like God, knowing good and evil."*

Genesis 3 then relates the thought process of the woman.

> *"When the woman saw that the fruit of the tree was good for food and pleasing to the eye, and also desirable for gaining wisdom, she took some and ate it. She also gave some to her husband, who was with her, and he ate it. Then the eyes of both of them were opened, and they realised they were naked; so they sewed fig leaves together and made coverings for themselves"* (Genesis 3:6-7).

The man and his wife began to see things from Satan's perspective. They could no longer see truth. They began to see something they have never seen before. The eyes of their minds were opened to understand the difference between right and wrong, correct and incorrect, good and evil but from Satan's corrupted perspective. Since that time, all fallen humanity has focused on what is right and wrong.

In Genesis, this is evident in the entirely different way Adam and his wife immediately saw each other. Previously, they had been naked and unashamed in each other's presence. After they ate of the fruit,

THE ENCOUNTER ON THE ROAD TO DAMASCUS

they looked at each other's nakedness and felt shame for the first time. Then they looked for a way to solve the problem themselves, grabbing the first thing they could find to cover themselves up, fig leaves! One of the effects of eating from the Tree of the Knowledge of Good and Evil is to see right and wrong and then try to solve the issue from our own flawed perspective.

The next thing they saw with their newly opened eyes was the Lord God himself or rather they heard him walking in the garden. They still recognised his presence but no longer saw him with the eyes of their hearts. Instead, they saw him with eyes that had opened as a result of eating from the wrong tree.

> *"Then the man and his wife heard the sound of the Lord God as he was walking in the garden in the cool of the day, and they hid from the Lord God among the trees of the garden.*
> *But the Lord God called to the man, "Where are you?" He answered, "I heard you in the garden, and I was afraid because I was naked; so I hid""* (Genesis 3:8-10).

The reaction by the man and the woman to the presence of God was to hide from him. When the Lord God questioned them, Adam admitted he was filled with terror at the presence of God because of his nakedness. His solution was to hide from God. Fallen man still recognises the presence of God but instead of responding to the life-giving nature of God, fallen man seeing things through the wrong eyes is terrified by God. Fallen man, seeking to try and solve the problem by his own efforts, ultimately ends up hiding from God.

All religion ever since has been about good and bad, right and wrong, man's futile attempts to solve their own problems man's way. More specifically, all religions become man's struggle to please their version of God. God is then seen through the wrong eyes because

CHAPTER III

we have eaten from the wrong tree. The first revelation Jesus brought to Saul was there is hope. When Jesus told Saul he was sending him to the Gentiles, it was to open their eyes, the eyes of their hearts, to see things as they truly are and not from Satan's corrupted wisdom.

The issue of seeing things through the wrong eyes can be traced throughout the story of the Old Testament.

When Moses came along, Israel was living out of the understanding of the wrong tree. Rules to live by was the only way they knew how to relate to God. The Lord God had given them the Ten Commandments which are based on the nature of God and his character, but they had been interpreted as rules to obey rather than a relationship to live by.

In Deuteronomy 29:4, Moses tells the people the root of their problem.

> *"Your eyes have seen all that the Lord did in Egypt to Pharaoh, to all his officials and to all his land. With your own eyes you saw those great trials, those signs and great wonders. But to this day the Lord has not given you a heart that understands or eyes that see or ears that hear."*

He was saying they had seen all those things with their physical eyes and mentally processed them, but their hearts had not "seen" what was real. Not that it was God's fault, their eyes were simply unable to see what was really happening. They did not see God, they only saw his actions.

Isaiah the prophet had an amazing vision of God's awesome holiness in his temple and was struck by his own humanity, his woeful inadequacy and his unworthiness. His behaviour was changed by this experience, but he does not change himself. God changes him in verses 6-7. Isaiah was given the opportunity to volunteer to go and serve on behalf of the Lord God. Rather than being commanded to go, he willingly offered to go.

Then God told the prophet what his whole ministry would consist of.

> "He said, "Go and tell this people:
>
> "'Be ever hearing, but never understanding; be ever seeing, but never perceiving.' Make the heart of this people calloused; make their ears dull and close their eyes. Otherwise they might see with their eyes, hear with their ears understand with their hearts, and turn and be healed"" (Isaiah 6:9-10).

The Lord was showing Isaiah these people saw and heard with dulled ears and fallen eyes darkened by Satan's corrupted wisdom rather than with the eyes of their hearts. They had the wrong eyes open. Their whole way of responding to God was all about laws and being right and wrong. The Lord told him his preaching would drive them more and more into their darkness.

The Lord was talking about the healing of their hearts, yet they were not going to see or hear with their hearts. The people were so established in their way of doing things that they would reject Isaiah and the words he was bringing. That is quite a calling, to be misunderstood!

Jesus quoted this same passage from Isaiah 6.

> "The disciples came to Jesus and asked, "Why do you speak to the people in parables?"
>
> He replied, "Because the knowledge of the mysteries of the kingdom of heaven has been given to you, but not to them. Whoever has will be given more, and they will have an abundance. Whoever does not have, even what they have will be taken from them. This is why I speak to them in parables:

CHAPTER III

"Though seeing, they do not see; though hearing, they do not hear or understand.
In them is fulfilled the prophecy of Isaiah:
"'You will be ever hearing but never understanding; you will be ever seeing but never perceiving. For this people's heart has become calloused; they hardly hear with their ears, and they have closed their eyes. Otherwise they might see with their eyes, hear with their ears, understand with their hearts and turn, and I would heal them.'
But blessed are your eyes because they see, and your ears because they hear. For truly I tell you, many prophets and righteous people longed to see what you see but did not see it, and to hear what you hear but did not hear it"
(Matthew 13:10-17).

Jesus uses stories, which we call parables, to get to the heart not the issues of right and wrong. These stories open people's hearts so they see with the eyes of their hearts. The disciples did not look like men with great potential from an intellectual perspective, however, their eyes and ears were being opened.

In verse 13, Jesus was saying that when we go back into our heads, we lose what has happened in our hearts. "Whoever has will be given more, and they will have an abundance. Whoever does not have, even what they have will be taken from them."

The focus of Moses, Isaiah and Jesus in these sayings was to open the eyes of people's hearts in order to restore our true identity, to heal our hearts with the love of God the Father so that we see and hear with our hearts as we were made to do in the first place and to restore to us what was lost in Eden.

In Acts 28:23-28, Paul had the opportunity to talk to many of the Jews in Rome. He explained to them that the revelation he was bringing would lead to the healing of their hearts.

> "They arranged to meet Paul on a certain day and came in even larger numbers to the place where he was staying. He witnessed to them from morning till evening, explaining about the kingdom of God, and from the Law of Moses and from the Prophets he tried to persuade them about Jesus. Some were convinced by what he said, but others would not believe. They disagreed among themselves and began to leave after Paul had made this final statement: "The Holy Spirit spoke the truth to your ancestors when he said through Isaiah the prophet:
> "'Go to this people and say,
> "You will be ever hearing but never understanding; you will be ever seeing but never perceiving." For this people's heart has become calloused; they hardly hear with their ears, and they have closed their eyes. Otherwise they might see with their eyes, hear with their ears, understand with their hearts and turn, and I would heal them.'
> "Therefore I want you to know that God's salvation has been sent to the Gentiles, and they will listen!"

In writing to the Church in Ephesus, Paul had prayed that the eyes of the heart may be enlightened (Eph. 1:17). Later in the letter, he urged them.

> So I tell you this, and insist on it in the Lord, that you must no longer live as the Gentiles do, in the futility of their thinking. They are darkened in their understanding and separated from the life of God because of the ignorance that is in them due to the hardening of their hearts. Having lost all sensitivity, they have given themselves over to sensuality so as to indulge in every kind of impurity, and they are

CHAPTER III

full of greed (Ephesians 4:17-19).

In the Fall recorded in Genesis 3, Adam and his wife's eyes to evaluate opened and the eyes of their hearts closed. Fallen man cannot see God as he really is. We are afraid and we hide from him, trying to cover ourselves with our false identities. Saul, in his calling by Jesus, was commissioned and sent to open the eyes of the hearts of his own people but specially the Gentiles.

CHAPTER IV

THE FOLLOWER OF THE WAY.

The light was brighter than the blazing light of the midday sun. It had been so dazzling and sudden, his eyes were hurting. Saul thought perhaps he had inadvertently looked into the eye of the sun itself and was struck with sun blindness. He was frightened. This was different than anything he had ever experienced before. He fell on his face, hands clutching at his eyes as if he was trying to uncover a blindfold. He heard his companions talking loudly. They had experienced something too, but he knew not what. He wondered if some evil demon had attacked him, yet this fear was different. Rather than the terror he knew resided in Satan's power, this fear felt different. As he lay there, a strange calmness surrounded him, and he was conscious of his heart racing within his chest.

Then it happened. He heard a voice speaking to him. He turned his head towards the sound trying to focus, but his eyes saw nothing except a mixture of dazzling darkness and light. The voice was familiar and spoke in his own language. The voice called him by name, not just once but twice. Instantly, he felt warm and accepted, the atmosphere created by the voice calming him inside. Am I dying? He thought. Is this what death feels like? How did the speaker know him by name? "Saul, Saul. Why are you persecuting me?" The speaker had asked, and in an instant,

CHAPTER IV

Saul knew he recognised the voice. His heart raced as if to burst out of his rib cage. This cannot be. This is impossible. He cannot be speaking to me. Surely, I am dead. No! No!

Mouth full of dust from the road and lips dry with terror, Saul asked, "Who are you Lord?" The reply was simple. "I am Jesus, whom you are persecuting. Are you going to keep on resisting the prodding I have been giving you?" In that moment, everything changed for Saul.

It was him. Saul could "see him", and he was very much alive. He was experiencing a supernatural encounter with someone he thought was dead. His physical eyes were blinded but as real and as clear as the noonday, he saw Jesus there beside him. In fact, it felt like Jesus was actually squatting down next to him as Saul lay there in the dirt. All sense of fear left, and he knew this was the one all those people he had arrested and condemned believed in. In spite of his actions, this Jesus was tenderly addressing him. Emotions swirled within him as tears welled up in his blind eyes.

As he lay there in the road, Jesus talked to him, poured out his heart for him and then told him gently to stand up. Saul raised himself to his knees. Jesus then said, "Now get up and go into the city, and you will be told what you must do."

The men traveling with him stood there speechless; they could hear the sound but did not see anyone. Saul very carefully got up from the ground, but when he opened his eyes, he could see nothing. He shuffled forward with hesitant steps, hands shooting out in all directions. He thought he would fall again, but someone grabbed his hand to steady him.

"What is going on? Are you hurt? Saul, look at us. What has happened? Can't you see?"

"Of course I can't see! But I am well, just take me to Damascus. Let's go to the house of Judas on Straight Street as planned. I need to rest, and I need to think, I think."

His followers led him by the hand into Damascus.

This was the beginning of the rest of his life. Saul would never be the same person again. For three days, he was blind and did not eat or drink anything. Yet those days were filled with visions, impressions and what he would later call revelations. He could not see a single thing with his own physical eyes, but he was experiencing an extraordinary transformation within him, seeing things in a new way. As if he was seeing with some sort of inner eyes of his heart, he was seeing everything differently. Things he thought he was once sure about, he was no longer sure about. He slept very little and had no desire to eat or drink. His companions were at a loss to know what to do with him.

An intense feeling of guilt weighed heavily on him. In the darkness of his blindness, images and sounds overwhelmed him. He saw the faces of many men and women, even children, that he had tortured in an attempt to get them to deny their faith in Jesus. Feeling the burden of his mistakes and actions like claws tearing at his heart, he tried to shut out their cries and groans. He could hear the words of the man known as John the Baptist, who years before had called the people to repent of their sins and show their genuine desire to turn to God. Saul, like many other Pharisees, had derided and ridiculed him.

Now he saw things differently. He still could hear the words that Jesus had said just a day or two ago. Jesus was sending him to both Jews and Gentiles to open their eyes and turn them from darkness to light and from the power of Satan to God. How could he do that when he was so lost in his own darkness? His eyes were now blind. He felt so acutely that what he had thought before, what he had done had been inspired by Satan's power. Just days ago, he thought he was doing this for God. Now, he saw it was the opposite. He had actually been persecuting this Jesus. How could he talk of forgiveness of sins and Gentiles being sanctified and made clean when he did not know this himself? He felt

CHAPTER IV

so unclean. He did not feel he had a place among those with faith.

Saul spent many hours crying, praying and confessing his sins and failure, his arrogance and ignorance. He remembered the people who went to hear the Baptist speak. They went to John at the River Jordan and were baptised as a sign of their longing for forgiveness and repentance; as a symbol of their washing and cleansing.

Saul wanted to know this washing and cleansing personally, to be free from the sin of the past. Strangely, he still felt the presence of the one who had apprehended him on the Damascus road and knew that he was nearby. Though his eyes were blinded, it was as if Jesus was sitting in the very room with him. He felt his presence and imagined he could see him. He wondered if indeed it was his imagination or something new, something more real than he had ever known. At times, he felt almost delirious with weakness and wondered if he was losing his mind. Other times, he felt more alive than he had ever felt as if every cell of his body was becoming fully alive. He began to see visions of the future, cities he knew, Tarsus, Jerusalem and even Rome. In these visions, it was as if people were beckoning him to come to them.

∽∼∽∼∽

On the third day of his arrival in the city, Saul had a particularly vivid vision along with the distinct impression that someone would come to visit him. In this trance-like vision, he felt he knew the man would be one of the very ones he had come to arrest and that the purpose of his coming would to be to restore his sight, Ananias. Saul 'saw' the man laying his hands upon him.

Like all the others in this small community, word would have reached Ananias of the persecution in Jerusalem and Judea. They had heard that the main instigator was one, Saul of Tarsus and he was on his way to Damascus to track down as many as he could find to take them as prisoners back to Jerusalem. There would have been rumours of some incident on the way, but none knew for sure what had happened. That same day, as he was working alone, Ananias experienced a vision in which Jesus himself called to him.

Luke tells us the story in Acts chapter 9.

"Ananias!

"Yes, Lord," he answered.

The Lord told him, "Go to the house of Judas on Straight Street and ask for a man from Tarsus named Saul, for he is praying. In a vision he has seen a man named Ananias come and place his hands on him to restore his sight."

"Lord," Ananias answered, "I have heard many reports about this man and all the harm he has done to your holy people in Jerusalem. And he has come here with authority from the chief priests to arrest all who call on your name."

But the Lord said to Ananias, "Go! This man is my chosen instrument to proclaim my name to the Gentiles and their kings and to the people of Israel. I will show him how much he must suffer for my name" (Acts 9:10-16).

Luke's account gives insight into the struggle that this must have been for Ananias who had to decide if the vision was indeed a heaven-sent vision or some bizarre trick of his imagination. Was it Satanic, sent as a trap for him to walk right into the hands of the persecutor general? Every vision and supernatural visitation evokes a questioning response from the recipient. Jesus spoke to him in this vision, whether Ananias had ever seen or heard Jesus speak is not known. It was not a full resurrection appearance as Saul had experienced, but it was vivid and real to Ananias. He stepped out in faith and believed and wisely asked a few questions. Jesus also told

CHAPTER IV

Ananias something about the calling that was upon Saul, his destiny and the personal cost of being his appointed messenger. He was a chosen instrument to proclaim the name of Jesus to the Gentiles and their kings and to the people of Israel. The local Followers of the Way in Damascus needed to hear that too as many would have been very afraid of him. Jesus said that he would show Saul how much he must suffer for his name.

Ananias went to the house of Judas on Straight Street. It is likely that he hesitated as he stood at the door before asking for admission. The doorkeeper may have recognised him and known him, perhaps not as a Follower of the Way, but certainly as a devout observer of the Law and highly respected by all the Jews as he was described. On hearing Ananias had come to visit Saul, they would quickly let him.

The house on Straight Street was the home of Judas who was likely one of the leaders of the Jewish community in Damascus, perhaps even a rabbi or the overseer of the synagogue. The home would have had a guest room and probably even a small bath house, often used by the Jews for ritual washing. Saul and his travelling companions had spent three nights there already.

∧∧⌵∧∧⌵∧∧

"You have a visitor, Saul. He says his name is Ananias and you are expecting him. Shall we let him in?"

The blind man turned his face, a face full of questions, and maybe for the first time in three days a ray of hope, to the sound of the voice.

"Yes, yes, please show him in." *Perhaps his arms reached out in the direction of where he heard movement. Ananias entered the room and looked at the man who was looking expectant, eyes darting from side to side seeking some light or clue.*

Ananias moved slowly towards Saul and reached out his hands. Perhaps there was a moment of hesitation, but he did it. He placed his hands upon Saul. Saul jumped slightly at the unseen touch. There was a pause as Ananias, whose heart would have been beating fast, gathered his composure and said,

"Brother Saul, the Lord--Jesus, who appeared to you on the road as you were coming here--has sent me so that you may see again and be filled with the Holy Spirit."

Ananias paused and then said, "Brother Saul, receive your sight!"

Saul clutched his eyes and rubbed them as tears flowed. Darkness was turning to light. He was coming out of the darkness of Satan's power and into the light of God.

"Immediately, something like scales fell from Saul's eyes, and he could see again (Acts 9:18)."

Then Ananias said, 'The God of our ancestors has chosen you to know his will and to see the Righteous One and to hear words from his mouth. You will be his witness to all people of what you have seen and heard. And now what are you waiting for? Get up, be baptised and wash your sins away, calling on his name' (Acts 22:14-16).

I imagine what followed may have been very much like this.

Saul stood to his feet and fixed his gaze on Ananias, looking deep into his eyes. They were soft and slightly anxious at the same time. Saul suddenly realised what a huge risk the man had taken to come to him,

CHAPTER IV

the great persecutor, of all people.

Saul smiled and nodded. "Me? Be baptised? Now? How do we do that and where?"

Ananias looked around. "Well," he said, "I know this place. In fact, Judas is a friend of ours. He is one of us and will be more than happy to show us where the ceremonial washing room is. It will serve perfectly for the purpose."

Saul looked surprised. "You mean he is Follower of... you know, him, Jesus?"

"Yes. He is a Follower of the Way. There are many more of us than you realise, but you will meet them soon."

Judas appeared with a few others. Together with Ananias, they led Saul through the back of the house to the small area reserved for bathing.

There were tiles on the walls and floor and benches around the edges for bathers to sit, typical of domestic Roman bath houses. Saul took off his clothes and looked at the pool of water. Ananias was already waist deep in the pool.

"Come on, Saul. Give me your hand, you are still a little unsteady." The two men stood in the water side by side.

"Brother Saul," Ananias asked, "do you turn from your former life of sin? Do you confess your need of forgiveness and do you turn to Jesus as your new Lord and saviour? Do you renounce Satan and all his works, and do you believe in your heart that Jesus is the Son of God who is risen from the dead and is alive?"

Saul nodded and then said, "Yes." This was all so new, and he would need to think about this, but at that moment his heart believed and was full of faith and he knew that was enough. He had seen Jesus. It was not hard to acknowledge him as his new Lord. He was ready to be washed in the water as a sign of being made clean and being forgiven.

"Then, brother Saul, I baptise you in the name of God who is our

Father and in the name of his Son Jesus our Lord and in the name of his Holy Spirit."

With that, Ananias gripped Saul's hands with one hand and placed another on his head and plunged him under the water. Those in the room smiled and clapped. There was a long pause. Judas the owner of the house looked at Ananias who seemed to be holding Saul under the water for longer than was usually practiced. Ananias looked back and grinned. There was a thrashing in the water, and suddenly Ananias let Saul go as he burst to the surface spitting out a mouthful of water. Everyone cheered as a bewildered Saul tried to speak. He uttered strange words in a language not heard before on earth. He looked puzzled and elated at the same time. Saul shook in the water, not from cold but from the heavy presence of the Holy Spirit who was being poured out all over him. After a few minutes, he spoke again, this time in his own language. "I feel so overwhelmed with the love of God. It is like waves of his love are being poured into my heart. I feel his Spirit speaking to me, and I know I am forgiven and I am loved. I feel like I am his son. This is wonderful." Saul threw his arms into the air and began to speak again, words tumbling out of his mouth in an unknown language.

In a few minutes, he stopped, rubbed his eyes, looked around the room at them and said, "I'm starving. I'd really like something to eat.

Luke's account continues in Acts 9.

"Saul spent several days with the disciples in Damascus. At once he began to preach in the synagogues that Jesus is the Son of God. All those who heard him were astonished and asked, "Isn't he the man who raised havoc in Jerusalem among those who call on this name? And hasn't he come

CHAPTER IV

here to take them as prisoners to the chief priests?" Yet Saul grew more and more powerful and baffled the Jews living in Damascus by proving that Jesus is the Christ" (Acts 9:19-22).

Once Saul met Jesus, he needed no further convincing that he was indeed the Messiah the Jews were anticipating. The Greek speaking Jews used the word Christos, the Christ, to describe Jesus, which means the anointed one. Saul was convinced that Jesus was the son of God. This was a huge change in Saul's thinking. For a Pharisee or any other Jew to say that Jesus was the 'Son' of God, to say that God had a son, was blasphemous. For God to have a son would mean that God was a father. Traditionally, the Jews had not used this word to describe the Lord God. God was Yahweh. Their fear-based reverence for Yahweh meant they were afraid to utter his name. Whenever they read his name in the Hebrew scriptures, they used the word Adonai, meaning the Lord. It was the very issue the Jewish leaders in Jerusalem arrested and tried Jesus for. Though not a sufficient cause to have him executed, when they presented Jesus to the Roman governor Pilate, they said he claimed to be the King of the Jews making the charge more political than theological.

For the grand persecutor to stand in the synagogues in Damascus and declare that he and they had been wrong about Jesus was astonishing, if not downright confusing. Every time he spoke, there were lots of questions and discussion. Saul was not holding back. He had only just recovered from his three days of blindness and he was preaching. This said a lot about his character, personality, energy and enthusiasm. Every day, he became stronger and stauncher in his preaching and explanations. Saul was used to arguing and debating. He was used to being right and pointing out who was wrong. This had been Saul's modus operandi as a Pharisee for years. It was as if without hardly pausing for breath, he transitioned from being the persecutor of the Followers of the Way to being, at the very least, the baffler of those who did not believe Jesus was the Way.

Years later, on trial before Agrippa in Acts 26, he reported what he actually said.

"I preached that they should repent and turn to God and demonstrate their repentance by their deeds" (Acts 26:20).

The language is very similar to John the Baptist's words as we have already discussed. It would indicate that perhaps Saul's initial preaching reflected John's preaching rather than what he would receive through revelation some years later. In his preaching, there was a recognition of the need to repent for sin and turn to God, but he added a thought at this point that was unusual and not typical of his later teaching. He said he looked for clear evidence that repentance had been genuine and had really taken place. The evidence he looked for was deeds and actions of perhaps contrition and change of behaviour. Typically, when genuine repentance has happened, the resulting change in behaviour and life is self-evident. To place this in the proclamation of the gospel at this point would indicate a more legalistic approach than was intended and suggests this is the converted Pharisee speaking who was very used to defining right and wrong and judging others by his own wisdom of who had and who had not demonstrated proper repentance. This feels like the approach which I have described as "wrong tree".

Whatever the intention, the result caused a huge reaction among the Jewish community in Damascus. Luke tells us in Acts that after many days, a conspiracy to kill Saul was hatched. It became apparent that the local Jews were trying to catch him and had set men watching at the city gates night and day in order to kill him. Somehow, the plot came to Saul's ears. Luke says the local believers

CHAPTER IV

hid Saul in order to save him and found a way to help him escape the city of Damascus by taking him up to the city and lowering him in a basket through an opening in the walls at night.

Saul's reputation and the news of what happened to him in Damascus must have filtered back to the authorities in Jerusalem and was likely a contributing factor in Saul's decision to not go up to Jerusalem to see those who were apostles before he was. In his letter to the Galatians, he said he instead went into Arabia.

CHAPTER V

THE PLACE OF REVELATION.

*H*e bounced precariously down the wall in the wicker basket. The men's whispered voices above grew silent. The rope jerked erratically as he was lowered to the ground. He reached the foot of the wall and listened intently in the darkness for any sounds, but all he heard was the bleating of a few goats off to his left. He climbed out of the basket and retrieved the bag that held a few of his belongings and some bread. Struggling to find a foothold that would take him to a path, Saul stumbled in the darkness. It was like being blind again. He found the path feeling his way forward. Much to his relief, the clouds soon cleared, and the moon shone making it a little easier to navigate the surrounding countryside.

An hour passed before he was far enough away from the city to relax. Thankfully, he had not been followed and began to feel safer. Saul walked until a rosy dawn fingered the hills in the far distance wondering where this path would take him. He skirted past the occasional farm and a village. Off to his right, he saw the sprawling buildings of a substantial country villa surrounded by vineyards and gave this place a wide pass. After some hours, he allowed himself to stop and rest and eat some food. With the sun higher in the sky, Saul held the bread in his hands and gave thanks to his new Lord for the food, his presence

CHAPTER V

with him and his safe escape from the city of Damascus. Having eaten, he got up and continued heading east towards Arabia.

∿∿∿

Arabia at that time was a territory to the east of the Roman province of Syria, not the place much further to the south known as Arabia today. It was a good place to lay low, reasonably civilised with scattered towns and communities but significantly outside the influence of Rome or Jerusalem. For Saul, Arabia was to become a three-year retreat in the wilderness where he would receive special input directly from Jesus.

The context in Galatians makes it clear that Saul received major revelation and visions directly from Jesus during this time in Arabia.

"I want you to know, brothers and sisters, that the gospel I preached is not of human origin. I did not receive it from any man, nor was I taught it; rather, I received it by revelation from Jesus Christ…When God, who set me apart from my mother's womb and called me by his grace, was pleased to reveal his Son in me so that I might preach him among the Gentiles, my immediate response was not to consult any human being" (Galatians 1:11-12, 15-16).

The nature of these revelations and visions was not detailed, yet throughout Saul's life, he regularly had divine encounters of a personal and significant nature. In great part, Saul rested his apostolic claim upon the divine visions and revelations given to him. To him, an apostle was what a prophet of the old testament had been — a man who had direct and personal communication with the Lord Jesus and received instruction immediately from him.

His visions began on the road to Damascus, where the risen

THE PLACE OF REVELATION

Christ had appeared to him. That experience had been so real to Saul that in 1 Corinthians 13, he counted it as one of the bonafide resurrection appearances of Jesus.

During the various missionary journeys undertaken by the apostle, he had several visions. Acts 16:9 records a night vision in which a man from Macedonia came and called him to come and help them. Whilst in Corinth, Acts 18:9 records,

"One night the Lord spoke to Paul in a vision: "Do not be afraid; keep on speaking, do not be silent. For I am with you, and no one is going to attack and harm you, because I have many people in this city."

There are also significant divine and angelic encounters when the apostle was being persecuted and would have been under great personal stress. In these situations, he received encouragement and comfort from God. In Acts 22:18, Paul describes another early appearance of Jesus soon after his conversion, urging him to flee Jerusalem for his safety. Many years later, following his trial before the Sanhedrin in Acts 23:11, Luke recorded that the following night the Lord stood near Paul and said, "Take courage! As you have testified about me in Jerusalem, so you must also testify in Rome."

In the midst of a dreadful storm that would eventually lead to a shipwreck on the shores of Malta, Paul experienced another vision. This time, an angel came to him. In an attempt to encourage the crew and passengers, he says,

"Last night an angel of the God to whom I belong and whom I serve stood beside me and said, 'Do not be afraid, Paul. You must stand trial before Caesar; and God has graciously given you the lives of all who sail with you'" (Acts 27:23-24).

One of his visits to Jerusalem was a direct result of revelation

CHAPTER V

he received.

> *"Then after fourteen years, I went up again to Jerusalem, this time with Barnabas. I took Titus along also. I went in response to a revelation and, meeting privately with those esteemed as leaders" (Galatians 2:1-2).*

In 2 Corinthians, where he is reluctantly reminding the Corinthians of the genuine nature of his apostolic appointment and calling, he relates an incident that had occurred fourteen years before. Most commentators believe this is Paul modestly talking about his own experience. He writes,

> *"I will go on to visions and revelations from the Lord. I know a man in Christ who fourteen years ago was caught up to the third heaven. Whether it was in the body or out of the body I do not know—God knows. And I know that this man… was caught up to paradise and heard inexpressible things, things that no one is permitted to tell"*
> *(2 Corinthians 12:1-4).*

If this is indeed his own experience, the fact that he places this as fourteen years earlier might place this in his Arabian experience.

The time in Arabia was a very significant time for Saul. It was both transitional and transformational.

Saul's radical conversion changed his whole worldview overnight. The change from pharisaical thinking would have been shocking. Along with the unexpected encounter with Jesus came the realisation that the very people he had been persecuting, torturing and murdering were now the ones who helped care for him in Damascus. Indeed, by harbouring him amongst them, they continued to put their own lives at risk. Time alone in Arabia would have been an excellent time to take stock of these events.

When Saul arrived in Arabia, he was newly converted and no

THE PLACE OF REVELATION

doubt reflected on his new situation and the nature of forgiveness.

Saul had not received much instruction in his new-found faith. He had not met any of the apostles or leaders. He had only met a few of the Followers of the Way in Damascus and picked up rudimentary elements of his new faith. He had not heard Jesus teach, as far as we know, though he did have an extensive knowledge of the Old Testament.

One of the major revelations Saul received quite early in his journey would have been about the true nature of what happened when Jesus died on the cross. His meeting with Jesus on the way to Damascus had convinced him of the truth of his resurrection. It was more than a vision, it was a real encounter. This would have had a profound effect on Saul. If he had indeed witnessed the crucifixion as I have suggested, it would be a vivid picture in his mind.[1]

As the years unfolded, Saul began to preach specifically about the cross. It was a distinct message of his, becoming the essence of the gospel he preached. Christ died for our sins and rose from the dead for our salvation (1 Corinthians 15:1-4). Saul's gospel was faith in the work of Jesus on the cross and nothing else. None of the other writers of the New Testament or the apostles whose preaching we read about in the early chapters of Acts preached this gospel of the cross until they learned about it from Saul whom they knew as Paul.

The word in the New Testament that is translated into English as 'cross' is 'stauros'. In the gospels, this word is used seventeen times collectively by the four writers in their accounts of Christ's crucifixion to describe the instrument of execution. In context, the 'stauros' was the instrument of torture and death the Romans had invented and used to execute criminals. In Paul's writings, he used the same word ten times.

No writer used the word outside of the Gospels, except Paul.

CHAPTER V

"The apostolic preaching of the cross" was a phrase Paul received by revelation from Jesus and was unique to him.

The other word that is translated cross is 'ksolon' which can also mean "club," "tree," "cross," "stocks," "wood." When the apostle Peter used the word 'cross' in I Peter 2:24, he used 'ksolon' instead of 'stauros'. Interestingly, in Revelation, 'ksolon' was used five times and four of them are related to the tree of life. More important than the translation of the word itself is to recognise the apparent lack of understanding of its significance by writers other than Paul. Other writers had no understanding that Jesus' death on the cross was the means by which God had solved the problem of sin. This significance of the cross was revealed through the apostle Paul alone.

Paul's revelation and understanding of Jesus' crucifixion was in stark contrast to that of Peter. For Peter, the crucifixion was all about accusation and condemnation which required Jewish repentance before God could establish his earthly kingdom as seen in his preaching in Acts 2:36 and 4:10. For Paul, Jesus' crucifixion was the message of salvation not an event to be repented of but an event to boast about continually (1 Cor. 1:23, 2:2; 2 Cor. 13:4; Gal. 2:20, 3:1, 6:14). For Paul, Jesus' crucifixion and resurrection were his victory over sin and death.

The early sermons preached by Peter and the other apostles recorded in Acts focus on the amazing fact that God raised Jesus from the dead. The references to the death of Jesus made by Peter and the others focused on accusation of the complicity by both the Jewish authorities and the Romans rather than what God did in the death of his son. By contrast, they highlighted the work of God in raising Jesus to life as proof that he was the Son of God. The response they called for was repentance and turning to God and the evidence of their repentance was baptism.

THE PLACE OF REVELATION

Paul did not take this approach. In 1 Corinthians 1:17, Paul says,
"For Christ did not send me to baptise, but to preach the gospel, not with wisdom and eloquence, lest the cross of Christ be emptied of its power. For the message of the cross is foolishness to those who are perishing, but to us who are being saved it is the power of God."

On Paul's first missionary journey, his first sermon was to Jews in the synagogue in Pisidian, Antioch (Acts 13). Paul began in a similar way as Peter in his early sermons in Acts. However, the conclusion he draws is different. Jesus death and resurrection not only prove him to be the promised Messiah, the Son of God but through his death there is also forgiveness of sins.

"Therefore, my friends, I want you to know that through Jesus the forgiveness of sins is proclaimed to you. Through him everyone who believes is set free from every sin, a justification you were not able to obtain under the law of Moses (Acts 13:38-39).

In the last paragraph, Paul clearly stated his revelation of what happened in the death of Jesus on the cross. Forgiveness of sins is given to those who believe. Stating this was not possible under the law of Moses, Paul clearly showed that his message was different from the message of John the Baptist.

To Paul, the 'word' of the cross, that is the doctrine of the cross was foolishness to unbelievers but for those who were being saved, it was the very power of God at work (1 Cor. 1:18). The doctrine of the cross was that Jesus died for our sins and solved the sin problem once and for all. This proved to be a stumbling block to those who would preach the necessity of circumcision and keeping the law of Moses for salvation.

Paul's boast was the work of the cross not man's self-effort (Gal.

CHAPTER V

6:14). He saw that both Jews and Gentiles would be united and reconciled to each other and to God by the work of Jesus on the cross. He later explained this in his letter to the Ephesians in Chapter 2 verse 16.

Paul also received revelation and fully understood the suffering that Jesus experienced on the cross. He saw how Jesus embraced that suffering on behalf of mankind. Paul saw how Jesus humbled himself in dying on the cross as he wrote in Philippians 2:8. It was so important to Paul that nothing be added to or taken away from this revelation of Jesus' work. Those who oppose this teaching he declared make themselves enemies of the cross (Phil. 3:18).

Paul saw that God the Father reconciled man to himself and made peace with mankind through the shedding of Jesus' blood on the cross. Quite literally, the cross was the crux of all history. The event to which all history was working toward since the fall of man in the garden of Eden was the death of Jesus on the cross. The debt against man which had separated mankind from God was cancelled by the cross. It was as if the debt was nailed to the cross, Paul said in Colossians 2:14. The vivid language Paul used suggests strongly that he had personal knowledge of the events of the crucifixion.

Closely associated with the cross of Christ is the "blood of Christ", and again it is with Paul that we find the greatest emphasis. Jesus had explained the significance of his blood to the disciples at the last supper as mentioned in Matthew 26:28, Mark 14:24 and Luke 22:20. Clearly, they did not understand it, for they did not preach it. We do not discover the significance of the "blood of Christ" until Paul wrote about it after his salvation. Only after Paul's teaching did the other apostles mention it.

Paul learnt the significance of Christ's work on the cross by direct revelation from the risen, glorified Christ.

THE PLACE OF REVELATION

In his letters, he taught redemption, propitiation, reconciliation, justification, and the blood of Christ. All these great truths are understood through the work of Jesus on the cross. Paul's gospel, that Christ died for our sins and rose from the dead was a "secret" God had kept (Rom. 16:25). Paul himself several times described the gospel he preached as his gospel (Romans 2:16; 2 Timothy 2:8; Galatians 2:2).

Leon Morris in his book, *The Apostolic Preaching of the Cross* considered various aspects of the atonement, e.g., redemption, blood, propitiation, reconciliation, etc. He wrote, "When one reads the text and examines its scriptural index one is struck by the abundance of Pauline references and paucity of non-Pauline references to Christ's work on the cross. The obvious conclusion is that the revelation and explanation of the significance of Christ's work for salvation came from Paul."

Only later, through Paul's teaching, did Peter understand and write of the significance of Christ's death on the cross (1 Peter 1:18-19). Peter recognised the special wisdom given to Paul in this regard.

"Bear in mind that our Lord's patience means salvation, just as our dear brother Paul also wrote you with the wisdom that God gave him. He writes the same way in all his letters, speaking in them of these matters. His letters contain some things that are hard to understand, which ignorant and unstable people distort, as they do the other Scriptures, to their own destruction" (2 Peter 3:15-16).

As this revelation of the cross and the significance of the blood of Christ for forgiveness was revealed to him, Saul must have felt a deep sense of shame and guilt for the many who had suffered and died at his own hands in the weeks and months leading up to the Damascus road experience. His forgiveness did not eradicate his memories.

CHAPTER V

Years later, when writing his second letter to the church at Corinth, he reflected on the nature of suffering and hardship. His writing is profound because he saw the link between suffering and the need for comfort. In all his letters, Paul writes about what he has experienced. He began the letter,

"Praise be to the God and Father of our Lord Jesus Christ, the Father of compassion and the God of all comfort, who comforts us in all our troubles, so that we can comfort those in any trouble with the comfort we ourselves receive from God" (2 Corinthians 1:3-4).

Paul had experienced the comforting love of God the Father. Perhaps Saul first began to learn to receive comfort in his troubles during the time he spent in Arabia.

Saul would have had a deep need to deal with his memories and the pain associated with them. In our modern world, we see the connection between trauma and emotional and mental health and well-being. Whether that was remotely apparent to Saul, he undoubtedly would have had dark moments of deep regret if not self-loathing and personal accusation. These would certainly have been afflictions and troubles. Yet, when he writes as he does years later, it very clearly shows he had found the source of healing and recovery for his many and varied afflictions.

In this season of revelation, Saul saw that the work of the Son of God, Jesus, on the cross was initiated by God the Father. It was the kindness and love of God reaching out to man that brought about this reconciliation. It was initiated by the mercy and compassion of God for his estranged creation. He found God the father of our Lord Jesus Christ to be the Father of compassion and the God of all comfort.

The two terms are rich in meaning. Clearly, Saul had a revelation of the nature of the heart of God the Father as being one who has compassion. This word speaks of emotion in the heart of God the Father. Saul would have known the story in Exodus 34 where the Lord God reveals his glory to Moses.

> *"Then the Lord came down in the cloud and stood there with him and proclaimed his name, the Lord. And he passed in front of Moses, proclaiming, "The Lord, the Lord, the compassionate and gracious God, slow to anger, abounding in love and faithfulness, maintaining love to thousands, and forgiving wickedness, rebellion and sin..."* (Exodus 34:5-7).

In many ways, Saul had a similar experience. He had seen the glory of the risen Christ. Here in this passage, the Lord God describes himself to Moses as first and foremost, "the compassionate and gracious God". Saul's experience on the Damascus road, in the city and now in Arabia would have been very similar. Saul would have experienced God's amazing compassion, his kindness and grace, his slowness to be angry, his abundance of love, his committed faithfulness, his love that embraces thousands, his forgiveness for Saul's own personal wickedness, rebellion and sin. He would see this through the eyes of his heart which had opened. He would experience the comfort of God's love and the unconditional nature of his grace. Saul had done absolutely nothing to merit this. None of his works justified him receiving it, it was the Father's unconditional gift to him. This comforting, embracing Father of compassion would have deeply healed the wounds in Saul's heart.

The eye-opening revelation of the nature of God would have been in stark contrast to Saul's pharisaical mindset. The time in Arabia would have been a time of change in every way where Saul began to see things differently. He began to eat from the Tree of Life which

CHAPTER V

is a receiving of the gift of life from God the Father. This was an outpouring of love, grace, mercy, comfort and joy. In fact, all the treasures of heaven that God planned to give us, we receive by what Jesus has done for us. Saul began to see that what Jesus had done was incredible. He tried to put it in simple words, and the only ones that came were that we were "in him". We are in Christ.

The realisation dawned on Saul that God the Father had always planned to pour the treasures of heaven into his creation. He wanted to freely give us all the spiritual blessings of heaven and share them with us. This was made possible because we have been included in Jesus. Paul saw that before the creation of the world, the Father chose us to be united with his son Jesus. God had planned to have sons and daughters who would be special and set apart for him, blameless and guilt free. Saul saw this plan had been set in motion before anything existed. It had always existed in the heart of God. He saw that God's purpose was to always have offspring, sons whom he could lavish his love upon. He saw the Father wanted to view mankind as his sons, fully recognised as sons in every way. This love was the overriding motive in the heart of God.

He saw that the Father's heart was full of pleasure. That in his son Jesus, the eternal son of God, all this would come about. Saul saw that in Jesus we have redemption through his blood, the forgiveness of sins, in accordance with the riches of God's grace that he lavished on us. It was with wisdom and understanding, that God made known the mystery of his will. This was God's good pleasure purposed in Christ. All this would be fulfilled, and all things in heaven and on earth would be united in Christ. Paul would later write about this great revelation in his letter to the Ephesians.

Whatever the process and whenever it happened, by the time Saul began to preach "his gospel", it was rich with revelation that

THE PLACE OF REVELATION

no one else had seen up to that time, and it would change the way we relate to God and know him. Paul's gospel would be a major part of the returning to God of his sons and daughters.

CHAPTER VI

THE RETURN TO JERUSALEM.

Saul began the long journey back from Damascus to Jerusalem. He entered the dusty countryside as the city walls disappeared behind him and wondered if he would find the place where he had met Jesus. In many ways, it was not that important. Saul felt his presence with him all the time, and he was understanding more each day what it meant to be in Christ. As he approached what he thought was the place, he paused and looked around. Instead of fear and confusion, this time he was filled with an unspeakable sense of joy, gratitude and peace for the one who had met him that day. This new kingdom he had become part of was characterised by a deep sense of relationship with God the Father that made him righteous. Saul had a peace he could not find words to explain and a joy suffused with the Holy Spirit that kept bubbling up unexpectedly. He pressed onwards, journeying south.

There was a degree of apprehension that grew more acute each day. He wondered if anyone would recognise him. Would his former colleagues on the Sanhedrin Council track him down? What would 'they', those he had persecuted and tortured, say to him? It had only been about three years at most since he left the city, many would surely remember what he had done.

As he crossed the River Jordan back into Jewish territory, he began to hear more people speaking Aramaic. Saul wound his scarf around

THE RETURN TO JERUSALEM

his head and face to provide some degree of anonymity and keep the dust from his eyes. Even though he was not afraid, he felt the need to be wise and cautious. His plan was to make contact with some of the leaders. He had heard from the brothers in Damascus that the church in Jerusalem was much smaller than it had been and most people who were not locals had dispersed and gone back to their home cities and lands. Those who had remained were led by the Twelve, as they were called. One of the main leaders was a man called James who was in fact the brother of Jesus. Saul was surprised to hear this. He was aware that Jesus' mother had been in Jerusalem and witnessed his death, but there had been no talk of family when Jesus was arrested and crucified. He decided he would try and make contact with another of their main leaders, Cephas also known as Simon Peter, who was originally from Galilee. He wondered if he should try to meet the brother of Jesus, James. He was not sure how he would be received.

Word had been sent from Damascus some time ago that he had become a follower of Jesus, but he did not know what the reaction had been. Each step of the road up from Jericho was steep and hard. He met many others headed down the road, the other way. Some ignored him, and some stared quizzically at him. Perhaps it was his semi-disguised headgear or perhaps he was feeling paranoid. Saul smiled to himself. If they only knew.

As he approached the city, the crowds thickened. One of Psalms he knew so well ran through his mind.

> *"Who may ascend the mountain of the Lord?*
> *Who may stand in his holy place?*
> *The one who has clean hands and a pure heart,*
> *who does not trust in an idol*
> *or swear by a false god" (Psalm 24).*

When he had last left the city, his hands were dripping with the blood of the people he had tortured. His heart was certainly not pure.

CHAPTER VI

Now everything had changed, and he was going back to Jerusalem a very different man.

The gates were guarded by Roman soldiers as they had always been, but they were stopping people and checking some of the carts that were queuing to get in before dark. There were more guards than he expected, but there had been incidents. The Zealots had recently killed a soldier. He spotted several Pharisees conversing together, their prayer shawls draped over their heads. He looked away and then looked back. He knew them from before. One of them glanced in his direction and looked straight at him for a moment, but there was no obvious recognition. He walked on and turned to look back once more. The Pharisee stared at him intently, drawing the other's eyes towards him and pointing. Saul knew he had been spotted.

He made it through the gates without incident and melted into the back streets and alleys. He had been told by the brothers in Damascus where the leaders might be found. He turned into the street and stood in the shadows observing the house he was looking for. It was a two-story mansion or town house. The door was shut, the window partially shuttered. As he waited, the door opened, and two men came out and hurried down the street in the opposite direction. Saul went to the door and knocked tentatively. A young household maid came to the door and observed him with soft and gentle eyes. He asked if this was the right house to find Cephas. She paused and asked who he was. "Saul of Tarsus," he answered. Her eyes narrowed, and her smile disappeared. "Wait here," she said. In a few minutes, a man came and opened the door again. He looked at Saul steadily as if trying to see into his heart. "I am Cephas. We have been expecting you, you had better come in." Then he smiled broadly at Saul and added, "Welcome home, brother Saul."

THE RETURN TO JERUSALEM

How long Saul stayed in Arabia before returning to Damascus is not totally clear. The consensus from what he says in Galatians chapter 1 is that he stayed in Arabia for three years. What is clearer is that on his return from Arabia, he did not remain in Damascus long and soon went back to Jerusalem. In addition to this, there is also some confusion about how many visits he made to Jerusalem over the next few years. Several accounts of various things that happened in Jerusalem were mentioned in Acts and in Saul's own statements. It looks as if they may have all happened in the same visit but highlighted different things. I do not think it matters if we do not get the sequence exactly right. What matters is what emerged from these various visits.

In Galatians 1:18, writing as Paul he says,

"Then after three years, I went up to Jerusalem to get acquainted with Cephas and stayed with him fifteen days. I saw none of the other apostles—only James, the Lord's brother."

When Saul finally got around to going to Jerusalem, he was there initially for a very short space of fifteen days. On this visit, he met with Cephas. This is of course Simon Peter, one of the key leaders of the church in Jerusalem. Cephas is the Aramaic version of Peter's name and it is the same person. Paul in all his letters refers to Peter as Cephas. Names were often used interchangeably in this era. Saul was known initially by the Aramaic or Jewish version of his name. Paul was his Greek name which he adopted after travelling to Cyprus some years later.

The only other person ranked among the leaders other than the apostle Peter that Saul saw while in Jerusalem was James, who he describes as the brother of the Lord. James was not numbered among the twelve apostles and was apparently not a believer in Jesus until

CHAPTER VI

after the resurrection.

When Saul met James, they would have found that they had much in common. Neither had been followers of Jesus while he was alive, both came to faith sometime later. When writing to the church in Corinth, as already mentioned, Paul lists a number of resurrection appearances of Jesus. He specifically lists James along with himself.

"Then he appeared to James, then to all the apostles, and last of all he appeared to me also, as to one abnormally born" (1 Corinthians 15:8).

This is the only mention of a resurrection appearance to James. Common ground, it seems, for Saul and James as both had personal encounters with the Jesus after he rose from the dead. This is a tantalising glimpse of an appearance that we know nothing about how, when or where it took place.

Nevertheless, James came to faith and soon assumed a position of authority in the Jerusalem church. In Galatians 2:9, Paul acknowledged him as someone of some repute and a pillar of the community and seemed to number him among the apostles in the passage.

When Saul made his first visit to Jerusalem, the two men had the opportunity to become acquainted.

As said earlier, the visits to Jerusalem by Saul are difficult to sort out. The account of Saul's conversion in Acts 9 given by Luke confirmed that during his time in Jerusalem, Saul not only met Peter and James but was introduced to the wider group.

Perhaps his initial visit of two weeks was an opportunity to test the reaction of the church to what would have been a very significant development. Even if these events happened after Saul had been away in Arabia, the memory of the persecution would be raw and painful for many. Having the former persecutor among them would

THE RETURN TO JERUSALEM

have caused consternation and fear. It may have been that after an initial private visit, he returned soon after for what appeared to be a more public visit in which he was introduced to a wider group of believers in Jerusalem. It seems one of their number, Barnabas, took the initiative to connect Saul with the wider group in Jerusalem. This was the beginning of a friendship and significant working relationship between the two men. Luke's account reads:

"When he came to Jerusalem, he tried to join the disciples, but they were all afraid of him, not believing that he really was a disciple. But Barnabas took him and brought him to the apostles. He told them how Saul on his journey had seen the Lord and that the Lord had spoken to him, and how in Damascus he had preached fearlessly in the name of Jesus. So Saul stayed with them and moved about freely in Jerusalem, speaking boldly in the name of the Lord. He talked and debated with the Hellenistic Jews, but they tried to kill him. When the believers learned of this, they took him down to Caesarea and sent him off to Tarsus" (Acts 9:26-30).

Following his introductions to the church in Jerusalem which was supported and facilitated by his new friend Barnabas, Saul was eager to share his revelations. Inevitably, this would have involved a reconnection with the Hellenistic Jews in Jerusalem who would have remembered him well. He had numbered himself among them during the time of the death of Stephen. They would have been very curious to know why he had changed and what happened.

Paul, when on trial, said that during a visit to Jerusalem he had a vision in which Jesus spoke to him again. The events Paul described suggest this took place during his early meetings with the church in Jerusalem after his conversion and time in Arabia.

CHAPTER VI

> *"When I returned to Jerusalem and was praying at the temple, I fell into a trance and saw the Lord speaking to me. 'Quick!' he said. 'Leave Jerusalem immediately, because the people here will not accept your testimony about me.'*
>
> *"'Lord,' I replied, 'these people know that I went from one synagogue to another to imprison and beat those who believe in you. And when the blood of your martyr Stephen was shed, I stood there giving my approval and guarding the clothes of those who were killing him.'*
>
> *"Then the Lord said to me, 'Go; I will send you far away to the Gentiles'" (Acts 22:17-21).*

As a result of this vision, and with the encouragement of the leaders of the church in Jerusalem, Saul was advised to disappear for his own safety. He was taken down to Caesarea and put on a boat bound for his home town of Tarsus in Cilicia.

One of the most significant connections Saul made during his time in Jerusalem was with Barnabas. This man, like Saul, was a Hellenistic Jew but from Cyprus.

Barnabas operated as an encourager in his connection with Saul as it was him who eventually came alongside Saul and presented him to the somewhat cautious and fearful wider group of believers in Jerusalem.

The final piece of the puzzle that described Saul's movements after his visit to Jerusalem is found in Paul's letter to the Galatians where he described his early days as a follower of Jesus.

> *"Then I went to Syria and Cilicia. I was personally unknown to the churches of Judea that are in Christ. They only heard the report: "The man who formerly persecuted us is now preaching the faith he once tried to destroy."*

THE RETURN TO JERUSALEM

And they praised God because of me" (Galatians 1:21-24).

Saul went back to his home town of Tarsus and stayed there for many years. The inference in this statement by him in the letter to the Galatians may indicate that he preached and evangelised there as well.

CHAPTER VII

THE TEACHER IN ANTIOCH.

*S*aul finished the final stitch in the flap of the tent and sat back. He looked at his work with some degree of satisfaction. The whole order had taken many weeks to complete, but there were now over fifty tents completed for this particular order. It was good business. Saul had learned this skill from his father and had been working in the tent making business for years. He knew from experience that he would be paid, as the contractor was the commander of the city garrison. The Roman army seemed to have an endless need for good quality tents. Out to the east, somewhere near the frontier with Persia, there was some sort of expedition going on. The Romans needed tents and paid for craftsmanship and experience. Known as the best tent maker in Tarsus, he was their man, and as a Roman citizen, Saul was certain the Roman authorities would come to him first and they would pay him.

His father and mother were gone now, and he was very much working on his own. It had been some years since he had moved back to Tarsus from Jerusalem. He reflected back over the last few years and wondered about his life. He had a deep sense of the presence of God with him all the time. He knew he had been given a commission by Jesus to preach and to take the revelations he had received to the non-Jewish, Gentile world, but he was still waiting. He took the opportunity to preach

THE TEACHER IN ANTIOCH

whenever he could, but he had no sense his moment to begin had arrived. Some days, he wondered if he had imagined it. He had talked about what happened to him on the way to Damascus and in Arabia with some of his friends, and they listened politely at first, but mostly they thought he was mad! He struggled sometimes to try and make things happen, but there was no anointing on it. The harder he tried and the more effort he put into it, the less joy there was and nothing seemed to come as a result. So, he waited. The months had turned into years, still he waited.

He put down the last of the completed tents and looked out through the doorway of the workshop. A man was walking slowly down the street and stopped a few shops down from Saul's. He was obviously looking for something. The shopkeeper he was talking to pointed towards Saul's shop and the man turned and headed in his direction. Saul shaded his eyes from the glare of the street and tried to focus on the stranger. As he looked, his heart began to beat strongly, a sense of excitement stirred him. He felt the presence of the Holy Spirit all over him. The man's voice called out at the front of the shop. "Saul? Is there someone here called Saul?"

Saul recognised the voice and his face broke into a broad smile. "Yes, yes, I'm here. Come in, Joseph Barnabas! You are most welcome. What are you doing here?"

"I'm looking for you, my friend. I need your help."

Saul knew, as surely has Barnabas had arrived, his time of waiting was over. A new day was about to begin.

∿∿∿

During these troubled early years for the Church there was a scattering of many of the new believers. It seems many of the

CHAPTER VII

Hellenistic Jewish believers who had converted in the early years in Jerusalem took their new-found faith home with them. This is how Luke reported it in Acts,

> *"Now those who had been scattered by the persecution that broke out when Stephen was killed traveled as far as Phoenicia, Cyprus and Antioch, spreading the word only among Jews. Some of them, however, men from Cyprus and Cyrene, went to Antioch and began to speak to Greeks also, telling them the good news about the Lord Jesus. The Lord's hand was with them, and a great number of people believed and turned to the Lord. News of this reached the church in Jerusalem, and they sent Barnabas to Antioch. When he arrived, and saw what the grace of God had done, he was glad and encouraged them all to remain true to the Lord with all their hearts. He was a good man, full of the Holy Spirit and faith, and a great number of people were brought to the Lord" (Acts 11:19-24).*

The successful preaching of Christianity at Antioch to non-Jews led the church at Jerusalem to send Barnabas up to Antioch to oversee the developing church. Barnabas was the obvious choice of person to go to Antioch. He was a gifted leader and encourager and, by Luke's account, full of Holy Spirit anointing and faith. He was also a Cypriot by birth with a Hellenistic Jewish background as were many of the new converts in Antioch. Indeed, it is highly likely he may have known a number of them personally.

Founded near the end of the fourth century BC, Antioch was built on the eastern banks of the Orontes river in the Roman province of Syria. The city's geographical, military, and economic location benefited its occupants, particularly such features as the spice trade which flowed westward to the Roman empire along

THE TEACHER IN ANTIOCH

the old Silk Road from Persia and beyond in the east. Eventually, Antioch rivalled Alexandria in Egypt as the chief city of the East, and was also the main centre of Hellenistic Judaism at the beginning of the Christian era. Most of the urban development of Antioch was done during the Roman period when the city was one of the most important in the eastern Mediterranean area of Rome's empire. By the early part of the first century, nearly half a million people lived in Antioch and the surrounding countryside.

Barnabas spent time encouraging and strengthening the community of believers in Antioch, but he soon found the work was extensive and weighty and decided he needed help. It was perhaps one of his greatest qualities, recognising he did not have all the gifts himself and that he did not have to manage on his own. After some consideration, he felt himself coming back to an idea that had been growing in his heart. Thinking about Saul, whom he had met some years before in Jerusalem, he was convinced this was the prompting of the Holy Spirit and set off for Tarsus, some 220 kilometres away by road, to look for Saul.

After about a week of walking, Barnabas found Saul in Tarsus as expected, and Saul agreed to go with him back to Antioch.

> *"So for a whole year Barnabas and Saul met with the church and taught great numbers of people. The disciples were called Christians first at Antioch"* (Acts 11:26-27).

The two men spent a year teaching in Antioch among the believers who were being nicknamed Christians, literally "little Christs", perhaps as an indication of what they were being taught. One of the reoccurring themes in Paul's letters was the way Christians lived in a hostile word. In his letter to the Ephesians, written some years later, he wrote,

> *"So I tell you this, and insist on it in the Lord, that you*

must no longer live as the Gentiles do, in the futility of their thinking. They are darkened in their understanding and separated from the life of God because of the ignorance that is in them due to the hardening of their hearts. Having lost all sensitivity, they have given themselves over to sensuality so as to indulge in every kind of impurity, and they are full of greed.

That, however, is not the way of life you learned when you heard about Christ and were taught in him in accordance with the truth that is in Jesus. You were taught, with regard to your former way of life, to put off your old self, which is being corrupted by its deceitful desires; to be made new in the attitude of your minds; and to put on the new self, created to be like God in true righteousness and holiness." (Ephesians 4:17-24).

The church in Antioch had a visit from some men from the church in Jerusalem who had a prophetic gifting.

"During this time some prophets came down from Jerusalem to Antioch. One of them, named Agabus, stood up and through the Spirit predicted that a severe famine would spread over the entire Roman world. (This happened during the reign of Claudius.) The disciples, as each one was able, decided to provide help for the brothers and sisters living in Judea. This they did, sending their gift to the elders by Barnabas and Saul" (Acts 11:27-30).

Obviously, there was regular communication between the two centres of Christian activity, Jerusalem and Antioch. The two churches were quite different, not only in their location but also the makeup of the members. The Jerusalem church was predominantly Jewish in origin made up of people from Jerusalem, Judea and

THE TEACHER IN ANTIOCH

probably Galilee. Initially, the church had consisted also of Greek speaking Hellenistic Jews from many cities across the Roman Empire, but these people returned to their homes following the death of Stephen and the persecution that followed. As a result, many new Christian communities were established.

Antioch was one such centre. It was a much larger city than Jerusalem and the church there was consequently larger. Luke in Acts talked about large numbers of people being taught by Barnabas and Saul. There were many Greek speaking Jewish converts in the church but also an increasing number of converts from non-Jewish backgrounds, that is Gentile converts. The city was a cosmopolitan city with many cultures, particularly as it sat astride the major east-west trade route of the empire. There were safe roads in all directions and a port that was full of shipping that carried cargo and goods all over the Mediterranean Sea.

The arrival of the prophets from Jerusalem would have been welcomed by the church there, and we read that they listened carefully to Agabus' words. The fact that Luke tells his readers the predicted famine happened during the reign of the emperor Claudius is one of the historical anchor points that he used to ground his story in time. Most scholars place this around 44 AD, which would be consistent with Paul's comments in his letter to the Galatians about the passing of time since his conversion.

Most historians place the crucifixion of Jesus around 30 AD. Saul's conversion would probably have been in 33 or 34 AD. Barnabas and Saul's year in Antioch was most likely 43 AD.

The response of the church in Antioch to the anticipated famine was to gather together a gift to be sent to the church in Jerusalem. One of the other differences between the two churches was the financial situation. The Jerusalem church, from earlier references in

CHAPTER VII

Acts, also contained a number of widows and needy people. This may likely have been a result of the persecution of the church there and the subsequent hardships survivors endured. Having contributed a considerable sum of money when he was part of the Jerusalem church, this was already close to Barnabas's heart. So the two were sent up to Jerusalem with contributions from the church at Antioch for the relief of the poorer Christians in Judea.

No sooner had Barnabas and Saul arrived in Jerusalem than events took a turn for the worst. Acts 12 described a series of attacks on the church instigated by King Herod Agrippa 1, the father of the Herod Agrippa who would later hear Paul's trial in Acts 26. Saul would have been caught up in these events and may have witnessed a number of them personally.

The initial persecution by King Herod was the arrest of some who belonged to the church. His first target was James, the brother of John, the cousin of Jesus, and one of the original twelve apostles. He was arrested and put to death with the sword. This was met with approval by the Jewish authorities, so Herod proceeded to seize Peter also. This happened during the Festival of Unleavened Bread, that is the Passover.

Luke gives an account of the events as they unfolded.

> *"After arresting him, he put him in prison, handing him over to be guarded by four squads of four soldiers each. Herod intended to bring him out for public trial after the Passover. So Peter was kept in prison, but the church was earnestly praying to God for him.*
> *The night before Herod was to bring him to trial, Peter was sleeping between two soldiers, bound with two chains, and sentries stood guard at the entrance. Suddenly an angel of the Lord appeared, and a light shone in the cell.*

THE TEACHER IN ANTIOCH

He struck Peter on the side and woke him up. "Quick, get up!" he said, and the chains fell off Peter's wrists. Then the angel said to him, "Put on your clothes and sandals." And Peter did so. "Wrap your cloak around you and follow me," the angel told him. Peter followed him out of the prison, but he had no idea that what the angel was doing was really happening; he thought he was seeing a vision. They passed the first and second guards and came to the iron gate leading to the city. It opened for them by itself, and they went through it. When they had walked the length of one street, suddenly the angel left him. Then Peter came to himself and said, "Now I know without a doubt that the Lord has sent his angel and rescued me from Herod's clutches and from everything the Jewish people were hoping would happen."

When this had dawned on him, he went to the house of Mary the mother of John, also called Mark, where many people had gathered and were praying. Peter knocked at the outer entrance, and a servant named Rhoda came to answer the door. When she recognised Peter's voice, she was so overjoyed she ran back without opening it and exclaimed, "Peter is at the door!" "You're out of your mind," they told her. When she kept insisting that it was so, they said, "It must be his angel." But Peter kept on knocking, and when they opened the door and saw him, they were astonished. Peter motioned with his hand for them to be quiet and described how the Lord had brought him out of prison. "Tell James and the other brothers and sisters about this," he said, and then he left for another place. In the morning, there was no small commotion

CHAPTER VII

among the soldiers as to what had become of Peter. After Herod had a thorough search made for him and did not find him, he cross-examined the guards and ordered that they be executed" (Acts 12: 4-19).

The detailed nature of this story is extraordinary. It has the feel of an eyewitness account to it. My feeling is that quite probably Saul was at the prayer meeting and later told Luke of the events. If not Saul, it may well have been John Mark who appeared in the story.

We are told later that John Mark was Barnabas' cousin. He lived in a house in Jerusalem with his mother Mary. This would have made Mary an aunt of Barnabas. It would seem this was an obvious place for Barnabas and Saul to stay while in Jerusalem.

There has always been the thought that this house was in fact the location of the upper room where Jesus shared the Passover with his disciples before his arrest. I have wondered if this was the case as Mark's account of the last supper in Mark chapter 14, also has a strong eyewitness feel to it. It may also have been the place where the early followers of Jesus gathered and were together on the day of Pentecost when the Holy Spirit was poured out on them, though this involved 120 people.

Soon after this, Luke tells us Herod went from Judea to Caesarea and while he was there, he was suddenly struck down and died in a rather unpleasant way. Herod's death was interpreted as punishment for his blasphemous behaviour, typical of the way death and illness was seen during that time.

Luke went on to say that when Barnabas and Saul had finished their mission, they returned from Jerusalem, taking with them John also called Mark. This was the beginning of a long and interesting relationship between Saul and Mark.

Acts 13 begins with more detail about the makeup of the church

THE TEACHER IN ANTIOCH

in Antioch and what was happening in the community.

> *"Now in the church at Antioch there were prophets and teachers: Barnabas, Simeon called Niger, Lucius of Cyrene, Manaen who had been brought up with Herod the tetrarch) and Saul. While they were worshiping the Lord and fasting, the Holy Spirit said, "Set apart for me Barnabas and Saul for the work to which I have called them." So after they had fasted and prayed, they placed their hands on them and sent them off" (Acts 13:1-3).*

On their return from Jerusalem, no doubt Barnabas and Saul related all the events that had happened in Jerusalem. The death of James the brother of John would have been sobering news that would have again reminded people of the cost of their new faith as 'little Christs'. Seen by the early church as a privilege to suffer in this way, Saul would later experience himself the cost of being a follower of Jesus. Later when writing his second letter to the church in Corinth he said;

> *"But we have this treasure in jars of clay to show that this all-surpassing power is from God and not from us. We are hard pressed on every side, but not crushed; perplexed, but not in despair; persecuted, but not abandoned; struck down, but not destroyed. We always carry around in our body the death of Jesus, so that the life of Jesus may also be revealed in our body. For we who are alive are always being given over to death for Jesus' sake, so that his life may also be revealed in our mortal body. So then, death is at work in us, but life is at work in you. It is written: "I believed; therefore I have spoken." Since we have that same spirit of faith, we also believe and therefore speak, because we know that the one who raised the Lord Jesus*

CHAPTER VII

from the dead will also raise us with Jesus and present us with you to himself. All this is for your benefit, so that the grace that is reaching more and more people may cause thanksgiving to overflow to the glory of God. Therefore we do not lose heart. Though outwardly we are wasting away, yet inwardly we are being renewed day by day. For our light and momentary troubles are achieving for us an eternal glory that far outweighs them all. So we fix our eyes not on what is seen, but on what is unseen, since what is seen is temporary, but what is unseen is eternal" (2 Corinthians 4:7-18).

Typical of the makeup of the church, some of the leaders in the church at Antioch had a prophetic teaching gift. Barnabas and Saul are both mentioned. Then there was also a man called Lucius from Cyrene which was a province on the North African coast west of Alexandria. There was also a man called Simeon who was also called 'Niger', indicating he was probably of African origin. Finally, there was a man called Manaen who had some connection to the aristocratic Herod family. Nothing much is known about him except Luke says he had been "brought up with Herod the tetrarch." This Herod was the father of the one who had just died. When Luke wrote his gospel and then his second volume, the Acts of the Apostles, he said he carefully investigated everything, so it is highly probable this man was the source of much of the family history and detail that Luke gives about the Herod family.

As these men fasted and worshipped, they felt the Holy Spirit directing them to set apart two of their number for a specific ministry. For Barnabas and Saul, this was a confirmation of the calling that was already on their lives. We have seen this was already part of Saul's spiritual makeup. He had a calling on his life to take

THE TEACHER IN ANTIOCH

the gospel to the Gentiles since his encounter with Jesus outside Damascus. To some degree, he had begun to see this emerge in Antioch, but there was a new phase of activity led by the Spirit about to begin.

The ready response of the two men led the group to lay hands on them as a sign of their corporate blessing and approval. Then they were sent off on what was to become known as Paul's first missionary journey and decided to take John Mark with them. They went down to the port of Seleucia near Antioch and took a ship to the island of Cyprus, a short way off the coast. For Barnabas, this was familiar territory, he was going home.

CHAPTER VIII

THE CHURCH PLANTER.

*T*he ceremony was about to begin. Paul, as he was now known, and his two companions had been invited by their host. It was a ceremony Paul had witnessed a number of times before as he had grown up in Tarsus. This day, however, he would see it in a completely new way. The eyes of his heart would perceive a great revelation as he watched the familiar family event unfold.

Paul and his companions followed along as the father, the 'paterfamilias' or head of the family, led his family from their villa on the clifftop to the forum in the centre of the city. All the members of the family were in the procession. Even the younger children were accompanied by their guardians and trustees, educated household slaves whose specific job was to care for the male children in the family and be responsible for their preparation for adulthood. Many of the important citizens of the city and civic leaders accompanied the head of the family. The man was Lucius Sergius Paulus, Proconsul of Cyprus, who had been appointed by the Emperor Claudius. From the time of Claudius, his name has been mentioned on an inscription in Rome, and he was without doubt the most important official on the island.

The Proconsul arrived in the forum and climbed upon a raised platform to address the crowd. This was a special day for him and his family. It was the day he would officially declare which of his sons would be appointed his heir. The assembly craned their necks to see the sons of *the man. They were led forward by the guardian slaves and stood before their father. The oldest was a small, sickly looking lad who hung his head and could not look up. The father looked lovingly at him. Sadly, the older boy did not look as if he would be able to fulfil this role. The father's eyes moved to his second son, a strong robust looking youth. He called this boy forward to officially recognise him as his heir. The father wanted a strong, healthy heir who could work with and alongside him as father and son. An heir who would be able to manage the whole estate. This boy, even though he was a child and had been under the supervision of the guardian slaves, was about to be placed alongside his father as his son and heir. The ceremony was known as the son placing ceremony, referred to in Greek as 'huiothesia'.*

As the father called the healthy son forward, the boy stepped on to the stage and the father presented him to his family and friends. Beside the father, a toga and a ring lay on a table. As the two men stood facing the crowd, the paterfamilias placed his hand on his son's shoulder. With a loud voice, he called out, "This is my son. I love him, and I am proud of him." He took the toga which was known as the toga virillis and placed it around his son. He placed a signet ring on the young man's finger. From that day onwards, whenever the young man stamped a document with this ring, it would carry the full authority of his father.

The crowd clapped and cheered, while pressing forward to celebrate the boy and greet him. Paul stood transfixed at what he had witnessed. Though he had seen this before and had experienced it with his own father back in Tarsus, many years before, suddenly he saw it in a completely new light.

He saw that this was a beautiful picture of how God the Father of the Lord Jesus had placed us as his sons. How he speaks love and affirmation over his sons. Paul saw this was the result of what happened when we have been redeemed and bought back into relationship with God the Father.

CHAPTER VIII

Paul looked at the older, weaker son who had been passed over. He was hanging back. Paul's heart went out to the boy. He went over to him and spoke.

"You are a beloved son too, you know."

Tears filled the boy's eyes and then cascaded down his cheeks.

Paul continued, "When you and your family became Christians, God who is your real father, declared that you are a son because of what Jesus has done for you. Father God says of you that you are his beloved son, and he loves you and is proud of you too. He sees you clothed in a special robe of his love and righteousness. You are in his family. You are not excluded, you belong to him. You have always been his offspring just like the poet Aratus said in his poem Phaenomena. You remember that poem, don't you?"

The boy nodded his head and looked into Paul's eyes. He smiled as he let these words sink into his heart.

∿∿∿

Obviously, there is nothing in Acts about Paul witnessing this ceremony in Cyprus. But Paul knew this ceremony and it was in his thinking when he wrote to the Galatians sometime later.

Paul, Barnabas and John Mark had been staying in Paphos on the southwestern corner of the island of Cyprus. The door to the gospel had opened wide on the island.

> *"When they arrived at Salamis, they proclaimed the word of God in the Jewish synagogues. John was with them as their helper.*
>
> *They traveled through the whole island until they came to Paphos. There they met a Jewish sorcerer and false prophet named Bar-Jesus, who was an attendant of the proconsul,*

Sergius Paulus. The proconsul, an intelligent man, sent for Barnabas and Saul because he wanted to hear the word of God. But Elymas the sorcerer (for that is what his name means) opposed them and tried to turn the proconsul from the faith. Then Saul, who was also called Paul, filled with the Holy Spirit, looked straight at Elymas and said, "You are a child of the devil and an enemy of everything that is right! You are full of all kinds of deceit and trickery. Will you never stop perverting the right ways of the Lord? Now the hand of the Lord is against you. You are going to be blind for a time, not even able to see the light of the sun." Immediately mist and darkness came over him, and he groped about, seeking someone to lead him by the hand. When the proconsul saw what had happened, he believed, for he was amazed at the teaching about the Lord" (Acts 13:4-12).

At first glance, this story is quite shocking. It is a clear clash between darkness and light. The sorcerer Elymas was a false prophet whose words obviously impacted the proconsul Sergius Paulus. Seeing his influence over the official diminish, Elymas totally opposed what Barnabas and Paul were preaching. As a Jew, Elymas would have known the practice of sorcery was forbidden by Jewish law. In the confrontation with the man, Paul may have remembered his own violent opposition to the truth and how he had been struck blind on the way to Damascus. In Paul's strong challenge to Elymas, he spoke a word of rebuke over him that included a period of darkness just as Paul himself had experienced long ago. Elymas reacted as Paul had done and groped around for help. Witnessing this had a profound effect on the proconsul who became a believer. And, it had a profound effect on Elymas, no doubt. One can only wonder how long it took him to come to his senses and 'see the light'.

The presence of John Mark with Paul is an interesting connection. Without doubt, they would have talked about the experiences they had back in Jerusalem. It is this John Mark who is believed to have been the author of the Gospel of Mark. Whilst he doesn't feature himself in the Gospel narrative, there is one exception, which took place in a large house in Jerusalem with a large upstairs room that was used by Jesus to celebrate the Passover with his disciples. In verse 51 of Mark chapter 14, there is the curious mention of the young man who flees naked from the garden of Gethsemane. Many scholars have speculated that this was indeed a personal reference by the author to himself in his gospel. Some have even suggested it is like his signature, albeit anonymously. This literary device, whilst it may be used occasionally today, has never been identified in any other ancient literature.

This may be a romantic modern notion rather than a real reference by Mark to himself, but I believe it is extremely plausible to place Mark not only in the garden but also in the vicinity of the upper room story. Reading Mark chapter 14, we have some very specific information that has the feel of eyewitness testimony about it. The chapter has many small details that seem to have come from someone close to the events described.

The words Jesus spoke to his disciples at the table when he invests the Passover bread and wine with new meaning are recorded by Mark.

> *"While they were eating, Jesus took bread, and when he had given thanks, he broke it and gave it to his disciples, saying, "Take it; this is my body."*
> *Then he took a cup, and when he had given thanks, he gave it to them, and they all drank from it.*

"This is my blood of the covenant, which is poured out for many," he said to them. "Truly I tell you, I will not drink again from the fruit of the vine until that day when I drink it new in the kingdom of God" (Mark 14:22-25).

In his first letter to the Corinthian church, Paul later wrote about the Lord's Supper and referred to these events, following Mark's words very closely.

"For I received from the Lord what I also passed on to you: The Lord Jesus, on the night he was betrayed, took bread, and when he had given thanks, he broke it and said, "This is my body, which is for you; do this in remembrance of me." In the same way, after supper he took the cup, saying, "This cup is the new covenant in my blood; do this, whenever you drink it, in remembrance of me." For whenever you eat this bread and drink this cup, you proclaim the Lord's death until he comes" (1 Corinthians 11:23-26).

Perhaps the most significant part of Mark 14 is the description of what happened in the garden itself. Jesus is described as going alone to pray some way away from Peter, James and John. We are told that after Jesus had prayed and returned to the disciples, he found them all asleep. It raises the issue of the description of Jesus' prayer that is recorded. If all the disciples, including Peter, were asleep, how would they have known what he had prayed unless someone else was there in the garden listening and watching? I believe it was John Mark and that he was also the young man who flees naked from the garden.

What Mark does tell us about Jesus is seen in the way Jesus prayed and how he addressed God in prayer. Of the three Gospel writers who record Jesus praying in the garden, only Mark says

CHAPTER VIII

that Jesus addressed his father as Abba. This is the most intimate expression a small child used to speak to his father. It is similar to Papa or perhaps the somewhat overused expression, "Daddy". Abba is a term still used all over the Middle East by little children when addressing their fathers. It speaks of home, of love and affection, of closeness and belonging. It speaks of relationship and intimacy. When Jesus prayed, he enjoyed the very closest of connection with his Father. Mark says as he was "deeply distressed and troubled", and overwhelmed with sorrow, he fell to the ground. In this moment of deep pain and anguish, Jesus cried out to his Abba. The very resonance in the word would have comforted his aching heart. This is pure revelation Mark hears and records for us. It becomes deeply ingrained into the DNA of the early church as they realised they too were sons and daughters to the Father and could address the Father in such terms of intimacy as Jesus did. Paul's conversations with John Mark may have brought this into Paul's thinking as he uses this term in his letter to the Galatians.

> *"But when the time had fully come, God sent his Son, born of a woman, born under the law, to redeem those under the law, that we might receive the full rights of sons. Because you are sons, God sent the Spirit of his Son into our hearts, the Spirit who calls out, 'Abba, Father'"* (Galatians 4:4).

Soon after this, Paul and Barnabas decided to move on and planned to travel to the mainland. They took a ship from the harbour in Paphos and sailed for Perga in Pamphylia. When they arrived in Perga, John Mark decided to return to Jerusalem. This appears to have been a disappointment to Paul.

Paul and Barnabas strike inland from the coast, visiting the interior cities. Luke gives us his account.

> *"From Perga they went on to Pisidian Antioch. On the Sabbath they entered the synagogue and sat down. After the reading from the Law and the Prophets, the leaders of the synagogue sent word to them, saying, "Brothers, if you have a word of exhortation for the people, please speak." Standing up, Paul motioned with his hand and said: "Fellow Israelites and you Gentiles who worship God, listen to me!" (Acts 13:14-16).*

This invitation to address the synagogue was typically offered to visiting guest, especially those who were Pharisees. What follows is probably the fullest account of Paul's initial preaching to a group of Jews in a synagogue.

> *"The God of the people of Israel chose our ancestors; he made the people prosper during their stay in Egypt; with mighty power he led them out of that country; for about forty years he endured their conduct in the wilderness; and he overthrew seven nations in Canaan, giving their land to his people as their inheritance. All this took about 450 years. After this, God gave them judges until the time of Samuel the prophet. Then the people asked for a king, and he gave them Saul son of Kish, of the tribe of Benjamin, who ruled forty years. After removing Saul, he made David their king. God testified concerning him: 'I have found David son of Jesse, a man after my own heart; he will do everything I want him to do.'" (Acts 13:17-22).*

This introduction of starting with familiar stories from their history was a common device used by the apostles and Paul when addressing Jewish groups. They knew the stories and also the writings of the prophets. In speaking to Jews like this, there was a continual referencing to Scriptures that described the coming of

CHAPTER VIII

the messiah. These were then interpreted to refer to Jesus. In this sermon, Paul specifically mentioned King David and then declared Jesus as his descendant.

Paul then talked about John the Baptist's ministry which seemed to have had a widespread impact in the Jewish Diaspora such as in these cities far from Judea. Later, he would meet a group of John's followers in Ephesus. This was perhaps fifteen or more years after John was beheaded, though his influence was still widespread in Jewish circles. Paul continued,

> *"From this man's descendants God has brought to Israel the Saviour Jesus, as he promised. Before the coming of Jesus, John preached repentance and baptism to all the people of Israel. As John was completing his work, he said: 'Who do you suppose I am? I am not the one you are looking for. But there is one coming after me whose sandals I am not worthy to untie.'*
>
> *"Fellow children of Abraham and you God-fearing Gentiles, it is to us that this message of salvation has been sent. The people of Jerusalem and their rulers did not recognise Jesus, yet in condemning him they fulfilled the words of the prophets that are read every Sabbath. Though they found no proper ground for a death sentence, they asked Pilate to have him executed. When they had carried out all that was written about him, they took him down from the cross and laid him in a tomb. But God raised him from the dead, and for many days he was seen by those who had traveled with him from Galilee to Jerusalem. They are now his witnesses to our people"* (Acts 13:23-31).

Characteristically, Paul described the events around what happened to Jesus on the cross and his subsequent resurrection.

He then went on explain what really happened, what the message of the cross was, what God the Father did in these events.

> *"We tell you the good news: What God promised our ancestors he has fulfilled for us, their children, by raising up Jesus. As it is written in the second Psalm:*
> *"'You are my son, today I have become your father.'*
> *God raised him from the dead so that he will never be subject to decay. As God has said, "I will give you the holy and sure blessings promised to David.' So it is also stated elsewhere: "'You will not let your holy one see decay.'*
> *"Now when David had served God's purpose in his own generation, he fell asleep; he was buried with his ancestors and his body decayed. But the one whom God raised from the dead did not see decay. "Therefore, my friends, I want you to know that through Jesus the forgiveness of sins is proclaimed to you. Through him everyone who believes is set free from every sin, a justification you were not able to obtain under the law of Moses"* (Acts 13:32-39).

Here is Paul's message, the preaching of the cross that he received by revelation from Jesus. It consists of forgiveness of sins by Jesus, freedom from sin for those who believe and justification which is acceptance and life from God that was not possible by obeying the Law of Moses.

He concluded;

> *"Take care that what the prophets have said does not happen to you: "'Look, you scoffers, wonder and perish, for I am going to do something in your days that you would never believe, even if someone told you'"* (Acts 13:40-42).

Paul's preaching was very well received by his hearers.

> *"As Paul and Barnabas were leaving the synagogue, the*

CHAPTER VIII

people invited them to speak further about these things on the next Sabbath. When the congregation was dismissed, many of the Jews and devout converts to Judaism followed Paul and Barnabas, who talked with them and urged them to continue in the grace of God" (Acts 13:43).

For all of the next week, there were discussions and further teaching to groups and individuals by Paul and Barnabas, especially among those who were not Jewish but were attracted to the monotheism of Judaism. The whole city was talking about what happened and the teaching Paul was bringing. Paul was speaking as a man full of the Holy Spirit and anointed with revelation direct from God about Jesus.

"On the next Sabbath almost the whole city gathered to hear the word of the Lord. When the Jews saw the crowds, they were filled with jealousy. They began to contradict what Paul was saying and heaped abuse on him. Then Paul and Barnabas answered them boldly: "We had to speak the word of God to you first. Since you reject it and do not consider yourselves worthy of eternal life, we now turn to the Gentiles. For this is what the Lord has commanded us:

"'I have made you a light for the Gentiles, that you may bring salvation to the ends of the earth.'"

When the Gentiles heard this, they were glad and honoured the word of the Lord; and all who were appointed for eternal life believed. The word of the Lord spread through the whole region" (Acts 13:44-49).

The response by the Jewish authorities in Antioch in Pisidia was a mixture of jealousy, fear and a feeling that Paul and Barnabas where blaspheming. They used their status in the city to stir up opposition to the two, particularly inciting the God-fearing women of high standing and the leading men of the city. This resulted in personal attacks against Paul and Barnabas, and they were expelled from the city and the region. Paul and Barnabas shook the dust off their feet as a warning to the Jewish authorities and went to Iconium which was some distance away in Southern Galatia. Meanwhile, Luke says in spite of the expulsion of the ones who had brought them the gospel, the disciples in Antioch were filled with joy and with the Holy Spirit. A deposit of the life of God was left by Paul and Barnabas (Acts 13:50-52).

Once they arrived in Iconium, the two followed what was becoming a familiar pattern. They went into the local Jewish synagogue where they spoke so effectively, a great number of Jews and Greeks believed. However, not everyone welcomed their message, and the Jews who refused to believe stirred up other Gentiles against Paul and Barnabas by sowing doubt and confusion into their minds. Nonetheless, Paul and Barnabas spent considerable time there, speaking publicly and boldly about Jesus. Luke tells us the message of God's grace was confirmed by the miraculous signs and wonders that accompanied them. Their teaching and the miracles polarised the people of the city; some sided with the Jews, others with the apostles. This opposition came to a head when a plot hatched by the Gentiles and Jews to mistreat and stone them was discovered. The new believers warned Paul and Barnabas, and they fled to the Lycaonian cities of Lystra and Derbe and to the surrounding country, where they continued to preach the gospel. A young thriving church was left behind in Iconium as in Pisidian, Antioch (Acts 14:1-6).

The events that unfolded in Lystra and Derbe were different. These two cities did not have a Jewish community as there was no

CHAPTER VIII

mention of a synagogue. Paul and Barnabas pushed further into the southern part of Galatia away from the coastal cities. There were very few Jewish communities in these more remote inland cities. In Lystra, they encountered a man who was lame from birth and had never walked.

The lame man listened to Paul as he was speaking. Paul looking directly at him, saw that he had faith to be healed and called out, "Stand up on your feet!" At that, the man jumped up and began to walk.

When the crowd saw what Paul had done, they shouted in the Lycaonian language, "The gods have come down to us in human form!" Barnabas they called Zeus, and Paul they called Hermes because he was the chief speaker. The priest of Zeus, whose temple was just outside the city, brought bulls and wreaths to the city gates because he and the crowd wanted to offer sacrifices to them.

But when the apostles Barnabas and Paul heard of this, they tore their clothes and rushed out into the crowd, shouting: "Friends, why are you doing this? We too are only human, like you. We are bringing you good news, telling you to turn from these worthless things to the living God, who made the heavens and the earth and the sea and everything in them. In the past, he let all nations go their own way. Yet he has not left himself without testimony: He has shown kindness by giving you rain from heaven and crops in their seasons; he provides you with plenty of food and fills your hearts with joy." Even with these words, they had difficulty keeping the crowd from sacrificing to them (Acts 14:7-18).

The approach they took in speaking to a Gentile audience was quite different than a Jewish audience. There was an appeal to their general sense of religion and god consciousness. Some Jews who opposed the apostles came from Antioch and Iconium and spoke in opposition of Paul and Barnabas to the crowd, effectively winning them over. In the uproar that followed, Paul was specifically targeted and attacked. They stoned Paul and dragged him outside the city, leaving him for dead (Acts 14:19). Paul listed the various attacks and troubles he experienced in these years in chapter 11 of his second letter to the church in Corinth. Among a long list of other brutal experiences, he mentioned being stoned.

Luke tells us the new disciples in the city went out to him and gathered around him. They would have been praying for and seeking to revive him. Stoning was usually fatal but amazingly, Paul got up and went back into the city. It was decided they should move on for their safety, and the next day he and Barnabas left for Derbe leaving behind another small group of believers in Jesus who had responded to the gospel Paul had presented to them (Acts 14:20).

The visit to Derbe was more peaceful and less eventful. They preached the gospel in that city and won a large number of disciples. We are not told how long they remained in the city before they returned to Lystra, Iconium and Antioch (Acts 14:21).

We know from a brief summary of what Paul did after the initial introduction of the gospel in the cities, they strengthened the disciples encouraging them to remain true to the faith. Both Paul and Barnabas were experienced prophetic teachers having served the large church in Syrian Antioch for some time. Part of their teaching included a recognition that suffering and hardship were a part of the process of growing in the Christian life (Acts 14:22). In addition to teaching and instruction, they established some sort of leadership or oversight for the new communities.

CHAPTER VIII

> *"Paul and Barnabas appointed elders for them in each church and, with prayer and fasting, committed them to the Lord, in whom they had put their trust" (Acts 14:23).*

Moving on again they continued going through Pisidia, presumably preaching and establishing churches. They went also into Pamphylia and Perga where they preached the word. What is apparent in these few verses is Luke has only told us the headlines about the extent of the missionary activity of these two apostles. Their time in this area was extensive and a network of churches emerged as a result of their missionary activity. Paul and Barnabas went down to Attalia and with the work they had now completed, they sailed back to Antioch where they first departed.

Luke concludes chapter 14 by recounting their arrival back in Antioch.

> *"On arriving there, they gathered the church together and reported all that God had done through them and how he had opened a door of faith to the Gentiles. And they stayed there a long time with the disciples" (Acts 14:27-28).*

CHAPTER IX

THE COUNCIL OF JERUSALEM.

*T*he gathering of the believers in Antioch began that morning in a very typical way. Most of those who were recognised as leaders were there. Some were not able to attend because they were working and could not get free. They hoped to come later if and when their duties permitted. The Church in Antioch were expecting some men who had come from Jerusalem, but they had not yet arrived at the gathering.

It was always exciting when visitors came, especially when they came from Jerusalem. They would bring news from far and wide, particularly of how the message was spreading. Some who came had known Jesus personally and they were always encouraged to recount their conversations and experiences with Jesus. Many in Antioch had not met him personally when he had been alive, they only knew him as their Lord and Master after his resurrection. They, like all the believers, were expecting Jesus to return any day as he had promised.

Once, an older couple accompanied by their daughter, a woman in her late twenties, came from Galilee with quite a story to tell. The husband had been a ruler in the synagogue some years ago in Capernaum when his daughter had fallen seriously ill. They had heard about Jesus and how he had many times healed people, so they sent for him but by the time he arrived, their daughter was already dead.

They told how everyone was crying and wailing with grief because she

CHAPTER IX

was only twelve years old. The girl's father whose name was Jairus told them Jesus walked into the house, dismissed all the wailing mourners and went into the room where his daughter lay dead on her bed. As the church in Antioch listened enraptured, Jairus repeated the actual words Jesus had used "Talitha koum!" Then he translated as most people only knew Greek. He said the Aramaic phrase meant, "Little girl, I say to you, get up!" As the story unfolded, everyone realised that the little girl of whom he spoke was the woman with them in the meeting. This young woman had been raised from the dead by Jesus. There were tears in many people's eyes. A man who was not a believer burst into tears and asked how he could become a follower of the Way. The people in the room started to clap and cheer and there was great joy. They all gathered around, many of them wanting to talk with the young woman. Someone suggested they write the story down, and John Mark who was there agreed to do so. He was already thinking it would be a good idea to record the stories he was hearing.

This day there was quite a crowd gathered. They shared a meal together which they called a love feast and as they ate, they remembered Jesus. They broke the bread and shared it, speaking about the body of Jesus being broken for them and when they drank the wine, they rejoiced as they thought about his blood that washed their sins away. It was a very special moment. There was always lots of laughter and chatter as everyone enjoyed being together. It didn't seem to matter whether people were from a Jewish or Gentile background, or whether they were men or women or even slaves or freemen. They all were one in Christ. As Paul would say, they were all sons of God. One or the other of the teachers would speak or Paul would often talk about how important the death of Jesus on the cross was and how his blood had dealt with all their sins. 'Once and for all', he repeated.

This day, the visitors from Jerusalem arrived after the meal, but

THE COUNCIL OF JERUSALEM

nonetheless they were warmly welcomed. They seemed uncomfortable, as if they thought something was not right. They were asked to sit down next to some of the leaders including Simeon Niger, an African. But they refused to sit next to him, for some reason. It was every odd. As if a cloud had covered the sun, the atmosphere changed.

The visitors were invited to speak, and they began with the usual pleasantries bringing greetings from the true believers in Jerusalem. This caused people to sit up and look at them. The church in Jerusalem was usually never described in that manner. Perhaps it was just a figure of speech. The visitors said they were surprised there were so many non-Jewish people in the room. They also seem to be worried that the women were sitting with the men and not separated at the back. They indicated they wanted to pray and covered their heads with prayer shawls in the Jewish way. They looked around and seemed to disapprove of the fact that very few others did the same. Some of the Jewish believers looked uncomfortable and quickly covered their heads as they used to in the past.

One of them raised his hand and spoke on behalf of them all. He was obviously their spokesperson. Everyone grew quiet and waited to hear what he had to say.

"Brothers, men of Israel, thank you for your welcome. We are pleased to have this opportunity to speak to you. We bring an important message to you that will clarify some of the things you are doing which are not correct and ensure that you too are true believers as we are. Our purpose in coming is to stop you from engaging in some wrong practices that have become apparent among you."

The room grew very quiet as people looked on these men with concern. They wondered what these opening remarks meant. The man continued, "It is obvious to us that many of you are Gentiles, and therefore this means we are ritually unclean by being in the same room as you as far *as we Jewish believers are concerned. Our understanding of Moses' law says that we cannot eat with you which is why we did not attend your so called "love feast." We did not want to be defiled by that.*

All around the room, there was murmuring and shocked faces. The Jewish believers from Antioch looked embarrassed and awkward. One young man called Titus who was a Gentile believer spoke up.

"What are you saying, brothers? I was baptised after I believed. I have been washed. I have been sanctified. I have been made clean by the blood of Jesus. Isn't that enough?"

"No, it is not. I can see you are a Greek," the man answered, "I presume you are intact?"

"What are you talking about?" Titus asked.

The whole room was silent. People glanced back and forth between Titus and the man from Jerusalem. In the back of the room, another young man began to giggle until he was shushed by the people around him.

The man from Jerusalem stood as if to give himself more authority.

"You know exactly what I am talking about!"

There was a breathless silence in the room. No one spoke a word. Every eye was now on the man from Jerusalem who looked nervously at his colleagues. They nodded at him, as if urging him on.

"I presume you are uncircumcised, like all godless Gentiles?"

Stunned, Titus looked at the man. Finally, a grin spread across his face.

"That is absolutely none of your business!"

Nearly everyone in the room burst out laughing as the tension broke. Some of the Jewish believers looked at one another with questioning eyes.

The man from Jerusalem indignantly called for silence.

"This is exactly my business! Unless you are circumcised, according to the custom taught by Moses, you cannot be saved. You want to be a follower of Jesus, don't you? I am sure you want to be like Jesus. Well, you need to be circumcised just like he was, and we are, the true believers.

After all, Jesus was Jewish."

A shocked silence once again permeated the room.

At that moment, a short man who had been sitting at the side stood. Everyone turned and looked at him. "May I say something?" He asked.

"And who are you?" The man from Jerusalem demanded.

"I am Paul."

"Oh yes, we had heard of you. In fact, we prefer to call you Saul of Tarsus, not this Greek name you have adopted. What exactly do you have to say?"

∧∧∧⋃∧∧/∧∧

Luke's introduction to Acts chapter 15 is very understated.

"Certain people came down from Judea to Antioch and were teaching the believers: "Unless you are circumcised, according to the custom taught by Moses, you cannot be saved." This brought Paul and Barnabas into sharp dispute and debate with them" (Acts 15:1-2).

We can only imagine how Paul and Barnabas would have reacted and what was said in the sharp dispute and debate. The Bible is not afraid to hide things were there are disagreements and differences. What we are seeing at this point in the story is of the uttermost importance. Paul rightly saw this as a fundamental issue about the very nature of the Gospel he preached and the nature of the Gospel itself.

It is always sad when Christians disagree and there is a tendency to say we should accept everybody's personal views and ideas for the sake of unity. Some even say we must be tolerant and accommodating of different opinions for the good of all. It is one thing to try to accommodate and be tolerant but there comes a point, however, when revealed truth is being jettisoned or ignored

CHAPTER IX

that something must be done. Paul and Barnabas knew they had reached that point. In their eyes, what was at stake was this issue: Had what God done in Christ been sufficient?

Paul and Barnabas, along with some other believers, were appointed to go up to Jerusalem to see the apostles and elders about this question.

In his letter to the Galatians which was most likely written sometime later, Paul said in chapter 2 that he went up again to Jerusalem, this time with Barnabas and he also took Titus along. He said he went in response to a revelation. He did not say what that revelation was, but in the whole context of the first part of his letter to the Galatians, Paul wrote about having received direct revelation about the gospel directly from Jesus. It can be assumed that he was receiving confirmation from Jesus about the truth.

Luke says the church in Antioch sent them on their way, and as they travelled through Phoenicia and Samaria, they told how the Gentiles had been converted. This news made all the believers very glad. When they came to Jerusalem, they were welcomed by the church and the apostles and elders, to whom they reported everything God had done through them.

Rather than rush headlong into a heated public debate and confrontation, Paul said he and Barnabas had a private meeting with those esteemed as leaders. In this meeting, he presented to them the gospel he preached among the Gentiles.

Evident in Paul's account in Galatians 2 was a humility towards the leaders and respect for the leadership in Jerusalem. He said he wanted to be sure he was not running and had not been running his race in vain. They had a full discussion about the issue of circumcision of the Gentile converts which had been the major challenge presented to the Antioch church by the visitors from

THE COUNCIL OF JERUSALEM

Jerusalem. Paul related that not even Titus, who was with him, was compelled to be circumcised, even though he was a Greek.

In Galatians, he explained in strong words how the matter arose. In Paul's mind, these people were false believers who had infiltrated their ranks to spy on the freedom the Christians had in Christ Jesus and to make them slaves to the law. In the letter, he makes it very clear that they did not give in to them for a moment, so that the truth of the gospel might be preserved.

These are his words in Galatians,

"As for those who were held in high esteem—whatever they were makes no difference to me; God does not show favouritism—they added nothing to my message. On the contrary, they recognised that I had been entrusted with the task of preaching the gospel to the uncircumcised, just as Peter had been to the circumcised. For God, who was at work in Peter as an apostle to the circumcised, was also at work in me as an apostle to the Gentiles. James, Cephas and John, those esteemed as pillars, gave me and Barnabas the right hand of fellowship when they recognised the grace given to me. They agreed that we should go to the Gentiles, and they to the circumcised. All they asked was that we should continue to remember the poor, the very thing I had been eager to do all along" (Galatians 2:6-10).

As the church in Jerusalem gathered to discuss the issue, Luke tells us that some of the believers who belonged to the party of the Pharisees stood up and said, "The Gentiles must be circumcised and required to keep the law of Moses." Here was the heart of the problem. These believers were Jewish converts who still belonged to the party of the Pharisees. Their words were the same words used in Antioch that caused so much alarm and disagreement. These

CHAPTER IX

people had accepted the truth about Jesus, but it had not really changed them. They still owed their allegiance to the Pharisees and pharisaical thinking. Essentially, they were still living and eating from the wrong tree, the Tree of the Knowledge of Good and Evil.

The back story to this issue was the apparent complication for Jewish believers that arose when increasingly large numbers of Gentiles became Christians. For Jewish followers of Jesus, it was another thing altogether to literally break a lifelong habit of viewing Gentiles as ritually unclean. To meet with them, eat with them and relate to them as brothers was a very big change. It was only possible when their hearts and eyes were open by revelation to truth. As long as they tried to rationalise and impose their position on the newcomers, there would be conflict. It was trying to find answers by eating from the fruit of the wrong tree again. This is a practice that has plagued the church ever since.

Luke writes in Acts 15,

"The apostles and elders met to consider this question. After much discussion, Peter got up and addressed them: "Brothers, you know that some time ago God made a choice among you that the Gentiles might hear from my lips the message of the gospel and believe. God, who knows the heart, showed that he accepted them by giving the Holy Spirit to them, just as he did to us. He did not discriminate between us and them, for he purified their hearts by faith" (Acts 15:6-9).

Peter led the discussion, speaking from his own experience when he was in Joppa on the coast of Judea. As a Jewish follower of Jesus, he had to face the challenges of relating to Gentiles also. Luke recorded this incident in great detail in Acts 10 and 11, perhaps because this issue was a pivotal one for the early church. The fact that it was Peter who was the focus of the story is important and shows the high regard in которой he was held by the Jewish Christians.

Peter was in Joppa and in nearby Caesarea, a Roman centurion called Cornelius had a visit from an angel. While Peter's hosts prepared lunch, he indulged in a pre-lunch nap on the roof of the house.

> *Peter went up on the roof to pray. He became hungry and wanted something to eat, and while the meal was being prepared, he fell into a trance. He saw heaven opened and something like a large sheet being let down to earth by its four corners. It contained all kinds of four-footed animals, as well as reptiles and birds. Then a voice told him, "Get up, Peter. Kill and eat."*
>
> *"Surely not, Lord!" Peter replied. "I have never eaten anything impure or unclean."*
>
> *The voice spoke to him a second time, "Do not call anything impure that God has made clean."*
>
> *This happened three times, and immediately the sheet was taken back to heaven.*
>
> *While Peter was wondering about the meaning of the vision, the men sent by Cornelius found out where Simon's house was and stopped at the gate. They called out, asking if Simon who was known as Peter was staying there. While Peter was still thinking about the vision, the Spirit said to him, "Simon, three men are looking for you. So get up and go downstairs. Do not hesitate to go with them, for I have sent them" (Acts 10:10-20).*

This story shows the internal struggle Simon Peter was going through and how it took an angelic visitation, a supernatural dream and direct instruction by the Holy Spirit to get him to move.

The outcome of the visit Peter made to Cornelius is that Peter

CHAPTER IX

preached the gospel. Each part of the story was included by Luke for a reason. It is a story that is addressed to Jewish believers. They needed to see what the Spirit was doing as it would pave the way for what was about to happen. The gospel was about to be preached and spread all over the non-Jewish Gentile world. Everything was about to change.

Cornelius, described as a righteous and God-fearing man, was respected by all the Jewish people. In response to the angelic visit, he sent some of his servants to find Peter and bring him to his house.

Peter arrived at Cornelius' house and went inside where a large gathering of people, including Cornelius' relatives and close friends, waited. Peter said to them,

> *"You are well aware that it is against our law for a Jew to associate with or visit a Gentile. But God has shown me that I should not call anyone impure or unclean."*

Cornelius explained to Peter about the encounter with the angel and why he wanted Peter to come. He expressed great faith by recognising they were all there in the presence of God to listen to everything the Lord had commanded Peter to tell them.

Peter explained what God was doing in sending Jesus to announce the good news of peace. He reminded them of recent events in Galilee and Judea, how John baptised and then how God anointed Jesus of Nazareth with the Holy Spirit and power, and how he went around doing good and healing all who were under the power of the devil because God was with him. Peter then said,

> *"We are witnesses of everything he did in the country of the Jews and in Jerusalem. They killed him by hanging him on a cross, but God raised him from the dead on the third day and caused him to be seen. He was not seen by all the people, but by witnesses whom God had already chosen—*

by us who ate and drank with him after he rose from the dead. He commanded us to preach to the people and to testify that he is the one whom God appointed as judge of the living and the dead. All the prophets testify about him that everyone who believes in him receives forgiveness of sins through his name" (Acts 10:39-43).

While Peter was still speaking, the Holy Spirit came on all who listened to the message. Hearing them speaking in tongues and praising God, the Jewish believers who had come with Peter were amazed that the gift of the Holy Spirit had been poured out on the Gentiles. Peter told them no one could stand in the way of them being baptised with water since they had received the Holy Spirit just as the Jewish believers had, and they were all baptised in the name of Jesus Christ.

Word spread rapidly that the Gentiles had also received the word of God. But when Peter returned to Jerusalem, the circumcised believers criticised him, accusing him of going into the house of uncircumcised men and eating with them. In these passages, as if deliberately making a point for his readers, Luke describes the Jewish believers as 'circumcised' believers.

Peter told them the whole story and concluded by telling them how the Holy Spirit came upon them.

"As I began to speak, the Holy Spirit came on them as he had come on us at the beginning. Then I remembered what the Lord had said: 'John baptised with water, but you will be baptised with the Holy Spirit.' So if God gave them the same gift he gave us who believed in the Lord Jesus Christ, who was I to think that I could stand in God's way?"
When they heard this, they had no further objections and praised God, saying, "So then, even to Gentiles God has

CHAPTER IX

granted repentance that leads to life" (Acts 11:15-18).

As the council being held in Jerusalem listened to Peter's statements, they would have all remembered the events that had happened some years before. They would have remembered the door of the gospel had been opened by God to the Gentiles.

Peter's concluding remarks to the gathered leaders of the church and the other apostles was a magnificent statement. He succinctly summed up the whole problem for them of the Old Testament Law, how it was in reality a yoke the Jewish people could not carry, let alone put on the Gentile believers.

"Now then, why do you try to test God by putting on the necks of Gentiles a yoke that neither we nor our ancestors have been able to bear" (Acts 15:10)?

With one last great statement, he summed everything up.

"No! We believe it is through the grace of our Lord Jesus that we are saved, just as they are" (Acts 15:11).

This should have been the end of the matter. It was a foundational and concise apostolic statement that succinctly defined and stated the nature of salvation. It remains today a clear defining statement of Christian faith and doctrine. In saying this, Peter, clearly full of the Holy Spirit at that moment, was speaking with profound anointing.

After he had finished speaking, the gathered assembly listened in silence as Barnabas and Paul told them about the amazing miracles God had done among the Gentiles on their recent missionary travels in Cyprus and on the mainland as far north as southern Galatia.

When they finished speaking, James the brother of Jesus spoke up. He referred first to Peter's words but instead of calling him Peter, the name given him by Jesus, he calls him Simon. That may have been purely accidental, but it reads as if he was slightly dismissing him or relegating him to a lesser place. James sought to affirm Peter's description of how God had intervened to include the Gentiles as part of the chosen people by quoting from the prophecy of Amos.

Interestingly, his quotation is very close to the Septuagint version of the passage which was the Greek translation of the Hebrew. Where the Septuagint says, "the nations who bear my name," James says, "even all the Gentiles who bear my name." This is typical of how the New Testament writers used the Old Testament scriptures. Many times, their translations are not as tight or close to the original as modern-day commentators would be allowed to get away with. It is as if the writers used the Old Testament to say what they wanted it to say rather than what it actually said. Paul did this in his letters, and even Jesus did not always quote the Old Testament with a word for word translation. They were writing and speaking under the influence and inspiration of the Holy Spirit without any apology.

James made a unilateral pronouncement.

"It is my judgment, therefore, that we should not make it difficult for the Gentiles who are turning to God. Instead we should write to them, telling them to abstain from food polluted by idols, from sexual immorality, from the meat of strangled animals and from blood. For the law of Moses has been preached in every city from the earliest times and is read in the synagogues on every Sabbath" (Acts 15:19-21).

This statement seems unrelated to the discussions that had just been held by the leaders in Jerusalem. Where Peter had been speaking with the authority of an apostle, this pronouncement by James was very different. In many ways, it is a pastoral response to a pastoral situation rather than an apostolic decree. The conflict that had arisen was experienced at the level of most people in the church, in their relationships with each other, between Jewish believers and Gentile believers. It was as practical as could they eat together without compromise or at worst ritual contamination?

James' judgement may have been driven by a pastoral imperative and might have been an attempt to apply the principle, but it lacked the clarity of Peter's declaration.

It certainly said they should not make it difficult for Gentiles to turn to God, but it needed to be more specific. It needed to say circumcision was not a requirement for becoming a Christian nor obedience to Mosaic laws, but it stopped short of that. In some ways, James' response lacked the revelation Peter expressed in his statement. Whilst James was not a Pharisee in the way main proponents of the group who wanted to see Gentiles circumcised were, his response was characteristic of the Pharisees. It was a response driven by the Tree of the Knowledge of Good and Evil from Genesis 3. A response that defines everything as either good and acceptable behaviour and wrong or evil behaviour. When James' decision was put into a letter, it still did not get to the main point. Because the judgement of James lacked revelation, it would take someone else to bring this revelation in an apostolic way and get to the heart of the issue.

If it had been clearer, the problems that arose in Antioch may not have happened, and Paul may not have written his letter to the Galatians. However, that is hypothetical as the apostles and elders, with the whole church, agreed to send a letter to the church in Antioch. They decided to send some of their own men to Antioch with Paul and Barnabas. They chose Judas who was also called Barsabbas and Silas, men who were leaders among the believers. With them they sent the following letter:

> *The apostles and elders, your brothers. To the Gentile believers in Antioch, Syria and Cilicia:*
> *Greetings.*

THE COUNCIL OF JERUSALEM

We have heard that some went out from us without our authorisation and disturbed you, troubling your minds by what they said. So we all agreed to choose some men and send them to you with our dear friends Barnabas and Paul— men who have risked their lives for the name of our Lord Jesus Christ. Therefore, we are sending Judas and Silas to confirm by word of mouth what we are writing. It seemed good to the Holy Spirit and to us not to burden you with anything beyond the following requirements: You are to abstain from food sacrificed to idols, from blood, from the meat of strangled animals and from sexual immorality. You will do well to avoid these things.

Farewell.

The letter is distinctly pastoral in tone. There is a clear recognition that those who advocated circumcision for the Gentile believers did so on their own initiative and not with the support or authorisation of the Jerusalem leaders.

However, the letter is somewhat understated about the impact of these people and the suggestion is that it was the response of the Gentile believers in Antioch that was the main problem not the wrong teaching of the believers who were Pharisees. The Antioch church was "disturbed", their minds were troubled. It could almost be read that it was the Gentile believers who were at fault in their response. It would have helped if the letter had come straight out with it and said the teaching not only came without Jerusalem's authorisation, it was actually wrong! But even that would have needed to be done with conciliatory grace, otherwise it would also have been 'wrong tree'.

Armed with the letter from the Council of Jerusalem, the men were sent off and went north up to Antioch. When they arrived,

CHAPTER IX

they gathered the church together and delivered the letter. Luke says,

> *"The people read it and were glad for its encouraging message. Judas and Silas, who themselves were prophets, said much to encourage and strengthen the believers. After spending some time there, they were sent off by the believers with the blessing of peace to return to those who had sent them. But Paul and Barnabas remained in Antioch, where they and many others taught and preached the word of the Lord"* (Acts 15:23-35).

CHAPTER X

THE LONE VOICE.

*P*aul arrived late to the meal that he had been invited to by Manean. Both Jewish and Gentile believers regularly gathered at his house in Antioch to eat. He was comparatively wealthy given his connection with the Herod family and willingly shared with the others and hosted visitors. On the surface, all seemed to be going well. Peter himself came to Antioch and would share meals with the Gentile believers, eager to meet with everyone.

This meal, however, was different. Paul arrived and was shown into the triclinium, the large dining room where guests reclined around the table in the traditional Roman style. He noticed unexpected guests.

He was greeted by Manean and introduced to the visitors whom he instantly recognised. They were Jewish believers from Jerusalem who had opposed the lead taken at the Council to welcome Gentiles into the family of followers of Jesus without adopting the law of Moses, in particular circumcision. He looked around the room and saw Peter reclining next to the visitors, but he would not look Paul in the eye. Barnabas was also there looking awkward. There was no sign of Titus or Simeon Niger. In fact, Paul realised immediately that there was not one Gentile believer present. The room fell silent as he looked around at each of them.

"This is nice! A cosy party for just the boys, is it? What is going on here? Where's Titus and the others? Peter? Barnabas? Look at me! What

CHAPTER X

are you doing?"

"Calm down, Paul. Sit," said Manean, "let me explain. It's not what it looks like."

The senior of the visitors from Jerusalem raised his hand in the time-honoured way that said he wanted to speak.

"We are here with the full knowledge of James. He knows what we think, how we are zealous for the faith of our fathers and of our respect for Yeshua of Nazareth. We are his followers too. It is just that we believe it is necessary for us and all his followers to conduct themselves according to the law of Moses handed down to us for generations, to keep the precepts of the law and not to contaminate the purity of Yeshua's teaching with idolatrous, Gentile practices as some seem to be doing."

Paul's heart beat furiously; his mouth was dry and his eyes blazed.

"Peter, do you agree with this?"

Peter looked down at his food and shuffled uneasily on his couch. He sat up and swung his legs over the side and looked away. He was deeply embarrassed. "Answer me, Peter," demanded Paul.

Peter slowly turned and looked at Paul. All eyes were on him.

"They make a good point, Paul."

Paul could contain himself no longer. He shot back at Peter,

"Peter, how could you? You are a Jew, yet you live like a Gentile and not like a Jew. How is it then that you force Gentiles to follow Jewish customs? We, who are Jews by birth and not sinful Gentiles, know that a person is not justified by the works of the law, but by the faith of Jesus Christ. So we, too, have put our faith in Christ Jesus that we may be justified by the faith of Jesus and not by the works of the law. By the works of the law, no one will be justified."

It had been a busy few months since their return from the Council in Jerusalem, and Paul had used the time to continue to encourage the church to grow in their faith and learn to walk as Jesus walked trusting God their father in all things.

The issue of circumcision went away for a while, and everyone breathed a sigh of relief, especially the male Gentile believers. The church continued to grow. There was a sense of togetherness and belonging among them all. Peter came to visit after some months and moved very freely among the people. At times, it was hard to recognise that he was born a Jew. The level of freedom they enjoyed in this life of God in Jesus was wonderful. News came from time to time from the new churches around the coast and up into southern Galatia. All seemed to be well.

However, there were times when it was clear the issue was still not fully resolved in some people's minds.

> *"...before certain men came from James, he (Peter) used to eat with the Gentiles. But when they arrived, he began to draw back and separate himself from the Gentiles because he was afraid of those who belonged to the circumcision group. The other Jews joined him in his hypocrisy, so that by their hypocrisy even Barnabas was led astray"* (Galatians 2:12-13).

Who were these "certain men?" The traditional view has been that Paul's opponents were Jewish Christians, possibly former Pharisees who sought to "Judaise" the Gentile Christians of Antioch and further afield, even into Galatia and the new churches planted by Paul and Barnabas. William Barclay concludes that the troublers were probably Jewish Christians who also questioned the adequacy of both Paul's apostolic credentials and the gospel he preached. They apparently made circumcision the central issue among the

Gentile Christians because it was the classic symbol for one who was choosing to live like a Jew.

The specific motivation of these Jewish Christian opponents, was that they obviously viewed their cause as righteous and biblical. They seem to have used the Abraham and Sarah-Hagar stories to point to such a perspective, as numerous commentators have noted. When Paul wrote to the Galatians, he picked up this theme. The Judaisers considered it imperative that Gentiles be saved in continuity with Israel and in accord with the Law and customs of Moses by becoming Jewish converts.

Later in Acts 21, Luke tells readers what was being said about Paul by many Jewish believers. This is James and the Jerusalem leadership speaking.

> *"Then they said to Paul: "You see, brother, how many thousands of Jews have believed, and all of them are zealous for the law. They have been informed that you teach all the Jews who live among the Gentiles to turn away from Moses, telling them not to circumcise their children or live according to our customs. What shall we do" (Acts 21:20-22)?*

It appears that increasingly Paul was the target or focus for those who wanted to judaise the Gentile converts. Everything about Paul's ministry and preaching seemed to contradict what they believed. The confrontation he described in Antioch was a skirmish in the war that ensued between Paul and these men, and it would ultimately lead to his arrest in Jerusalem and trial before the Roman authorities years later.

Scholars who studied rabbinic and Jewish literature and writing from this time have identified a number of views current in the first century. It was an era referred to as Second Temple Judaism. These

Jewish Christians from the sect of the Pharisees expressed a concept of revelation typical of Second Temple Judaism.

According to this view, revelation flowed from the seat of authority which was Jerusalem where Rabbi Jesus had left his disciples, the Jerusalem apostles, to carry on the line of tradition. Paul would be seen by them as a "tanna", a rabbi who had broken the chain of Jewish traditions by not faithfully or accurately passing on the tradition. If they assumed that Paul was a pupil of the Jerusalem apostles, the Judaisers would apparently accuse him of failing in his duty to transmit the exact words of Jesus' tradition as it had been taught to Paul by the apostles. Such incompetence was viewed as one of the gravest offences according to ancient rabbinical rules. If this was what motivated the Judaisers then they had to correct Paul's breech of the Jesus tradition among the Gentiles. This is a highly plausible motive and would explain their dogged attacks on Paul over the coming years. Some have gone so far as to suggest that when Paul talked about a thorn in the flesh, a messenger from Satan in 2 Corinthians 12, he was referring to the Judaisers.

These Judaisers claimed to come to Antioch from James, the leader in Jerusalem. It is difficult to say how much of their behaviour was encouraged by James, nonetheless, Paul took a very strong stand against it. Whether James, the brother of Jesus understood the revelation Paul carried cannot be known for sure.

There is a letter named after James in the New Testament, but this has always been viewed with some concern and reservations since the earliest days of the church. Many of the early church fathers, whilst knowing the work, did not consider it to be inspired in the same way as the rest of the New Testament. Martin Luther, in the sixteenth century, described it as an "epistle of straw." In reading through the epistle, its writer has a strong emphasis on obedience

CHAPTER X

and good behaviour which are not in any way wrong itself but does not reflect the life and freedom Paul was so eager to promote in Antioch and in his letter to the Galatians and his other writings. I am left wondering if James' epistle exists as a testament to the early groups who were predominantly Jewish in background and who had some sort of allegiance to him and the style of Christianity he may have represented.

It must have been disappointing and discouraging for Paul to have to confront Peter, specifically for his compromising behaviour. Peter was after all a key figure in the early church and many would have been influenced by his actions. However, he had a history of behaving like this.

During his time as a disciple of Jesus, he was capable of great insight and revelation such as the time in Matthew's Gospel chapter 16 when Jesus asked his disciples, "Who do people say the Son of Man is?" After several answers, Simon Peter said, "You are the Messiah, the Son of the living God."

Jesus replied, "Blessed are you, Simon son of Jonah, for this was not revealed to you by flesh and blood, but by my Father in heaven."

A little later, Jesus began to explain to his disciples that he must go to Jerusalem and suffer many things and that he must be killed and on the third day be raised to life. At this point, Peter took him aside and rebuked him.

"Never, Lord!" he said. "This shall never happen to you!"
Jesus' reply to Peter was very direct.

"Get behind me, Satan! You are a stumbling block to me; you do not have in mind the concerns of God, but merely human concerns" (Matthew 16:13-23).

The pattern continued with the denial of Jesus by Peter after his arrest in the Garden of Gethsemane. Even though he had a history like this, Peter was still willing to change and receive grace and forgiveness. Many years later, when Peter wrote his first letter to the believers in many places including Galatia, he talked very movingly of the forgiveness and love of God the Father. He said to them that they,

> *"have been chosen according to the foreknowledge of God the Father, through the sanctifying work of the Spirit, to be obedient to Jesus Christ and sprinkled with his blood: Grace and peace be yours in abundance" (1 Peter 1:2).*

We are not told what happened after Paul's confrontation with Peter and the others. It is quite conceivable that the Judaisers moved on and travelled to Cilicia and beyond into Galatia spreading their version of the gospel.

Antioch was a major crossroads at the eastern end of the Mediterranean Sea. The overland route to Rome from the east and the south passed through Antioch. To the west of Antioch, the road led to Tarsus and the interior provinces such as Galatia and Cappadocia. To the northwest was the Black Sea and Pontus. Beyond were the Roman province known as Asia with the great city of Ephesus on the coast of the Aegean Sea. There would have been a steady flow of travellers through the city. The gospel had been preached in Syria and Cilicia by those who had been in Jerusalem on the day of Pentecost. Paul had spent many years in Tarsus, and there are suggestions that churches were established in that area also.

Another widely accepted view is that the Judaisers from Jerusalem visited the churches established by Paul on his first missionary journey in order to correct them and explain the 'true' nature of the gospel to them.

At some point, Paul wrote his letter to the Galatians. There has been endless debate over the years about when he actually wrote the letter and where he wrote it. The arguments are detailed and complex. Interestingly, the debate has never seriously doubted his authorship of the letter.

Some felt it was written before the Council of Jerusalem as he does not specifically mention this event. However, another group felt his comments in the beginning of Galatians 2 reflected this gathering. Now that I have worked with this story of his life, my opinion is that Galatians was written after the council and after the event just described in Antioch. My contention is that the Council of Jerusalem did not resolve the issue raised by the Judaisers at all. It is apparent to me that this group particularly targeted their opposition to Paul and to those places where Paul had been active such as Galatia.

My view is that Paul wrote the Letter to the Galatians sometime after the incident he mentioned in Antioch and before his second missionary journey began. His references to Barnabas in his letter would have been meaningful to the Galatians because of his involvement in their beginnings. At the start of Paul's second missionary journey, Luke recounts that a rift developed between Barnabas and Paul over the issue of Barnabas' cousin John Mark.

> *"Some time later Paul said to Barnabas, "Let us go back and visit the believers in all the towns where we preached the word of the Lord and see how they are doing." Barnabas wanted to take John, also called Mark, with them, but Paul did not think it wise to take him, because he had deserted them in Pamphylia and had not continued with them in the work. They had such a sharp disagreement that they parted company. Barnabas took Mark and sailed for Cyprus, but Paul chose Silas and left, commended by the believers to the grace of the Lord. He went through Syria*

and Cilicia, strengthening the churches" (Acts 15:36-41).

To have mentioned Barnabas as he does in his letter would have been surprising after the rift. Along with a number of eminent scholars far more learned than I, I believe Paul wrote the letter to the churches in Galatia while he was in Antioch, after the Council of Jerusalem and before his second missionary journey.

I have wondered what was the impetus that lead Paul to write the letter. In reading the letter, it is obvious Paul was addressing a number of issues that seemed to be levelled at him personally. One of the issues appeared to be a challenge about his authority as an apostle and the source of his teaching. The other challenge levelled against him was that he did not preach a correct gospel and that he deliberately neglected to encourage circumcision of Gentile converts.

CHAPTER XI

THE LETTER WRITER.

*P*aul was increasingly troubled by the reports that were filtering back to him in Antioch about the young churches in the interior. Visitors passing through talked about conflict among the Jewish believers and the many Gentile converts. In some places they were refusing to meet together at all. By all accounts, the visitors that caused so much confusion and trouble in Antioch had moved on and were doing the same wherever they went. He longed for news and began thinking seriously of going to see for himself. But that was the problem. His eyes were troubling him a lot lately, infection after infection that seemed to not get better. Travelling would not be advisable. He wished someone would join them who knew about these sorts of ailments and could give him advice and treatment. He began praying for a doctor to join his circle of associates as well as healing.

One day, Tychicus, one of Paul's young colleagues from the church in Antioch, brought him a letter, a scroll in fact that had been sealed and addressed to him personally. Tychicus was a scribe by profession, fluent in both Greek and Hebrew and often read to Paul when his eyes were troubling him.

"Would you like me to read it to you, Paul? I can see your eyes are playing up today," asked Tychicus.

"Thank you, dear boy, that would be a great help. Who is it from?"

"It says it is from a man called Timotheus of Lystra. Do you know him?"

"I am not sure," said Paul. "Let me think. I do remember when Barnabas and I first went there we met a young man called Timotheus -Timothy. He was just a youngster though. Yes, I do remember. He was one of the first to accept the message and join us. His mother, if I recall, was a Jewess. Lois, I think her name was, and I also remember another older lady. I think she was his grandmother, Eunice. All of them became followers of Jesus. I don't recall a father though. Yes, yes, I remember now, it's all coming back. His father was a Greek, but I think he had died and Timothy had been brought up as a Greek, even though by birth he was a Jew of course through his mother. He asked me at the time if I thought he should be circumcised as a Jew. I said it didn't make any difference, and it wasn't a requirement to be Follower of the Way. He needed to do nothing other than believe and receive the gift of grace and forgiveness that Jesus gives. I told him it was up to him if he wanted to be circumcised as a Jew or remain as he was as a Greek. It had absolutely nothing to do with becoming a follower of Jesus. I wonder what he is writing to me about?"

Tychicus had been glancing through the scroll as Paul spoke. His face took on a grave and serious expression.

"What is it, Tychicus? What has happened?"

Slowly, carefully, the scribe read the letter to Paul, allowing time for the words to sink. It was not good news from Lystra. Timothy was not sick. He was confused and was writing to Paul because he didn't know what else to do or who else to turn to. It appeared that it was being said that the gospel Paul had preached in Lystra and the other towns and cities throughout Galatia had been declared at best not the whole truth, at worst completely wrong. They were being told that Paul had misled them and that to be true believers, the Gentiles needed to be circumcised and start obeying the Mosaic Law.

When he got to the end of the letter, Tychicus rolled up the scroll and

CHAPTER XI

held it out. Paul took it in his hands and rolled it between his palms. Angry and frustrated and deeply sad, he was silent for long time. Then he spoke.

"Those foolish Galatians! Who has bewitched them?" He paused, looking pensive. "I know who is behind this. Those agitators who want to circumcise the Gentiles. I wish they would go the whole way and emasculate themselves! Tychicus, get a stylus and parchment. We are going to write a letter."

※

Paul realised the church faced a very significant challenge. It was a pivotal moment for the church and the future of what we call Christianity. Paul had been a lone voice for some time. However, there was a growing number of people who appreciated the issue, and a number of Jewish believers who had wavered were back on track, Peter for one. He and Paul had some long, heated discussions, but it was evident from the letters Peter later wrote that he saw the truth of the gospel.

The issue was quite simple. What was the gospel? Did it include circumcision and obedience to Jewish customs? Was the work of Jesus on the cross sufficient? What was the status therefore for those who had believed and where now "in Christ"? Paul's response to the Judaisers' challenge was to write a letter to the churches he had planted in Galatia. If indeed this letter was written from Antioch before his second missionary journey, then it was the first New Testament document written by anyone. The Gospels are believed to have been composed later in the early 60s AD. The Acts of the Apostles was written after Luke, who had not yet met Paul, wrote his Gospel. So Galatians is the earliest piece of Christian literature.

Whilst it was written to churches in southern Galatia, it was quickly recognised as instruction and truth for all Christians. Before long, it was circulated widely and most of the early churches had copies.

The themes Paul highlighted in Galatians are again taken up and developed in a number of his other letters, particularly Romans and Ephesians. The theme of the letter to Galatia describes fully the reality of being 'in Christ'. Being redeemed by Jesus results in us being placed in the position of sons and daughters to God the Father. Drawing together truth that he had received over a number of years by revelation from Jesus, Paul introduced his readers to the glorious truth of sonship which is our true identity and position in Christ. The importance of this letter cannot be overemphasised.

In Paul's opening statement, he launched straight into the issue of his own position and credentials as an apostle appointed by Jesus and the Father. The memory of his encounter with Jesus on the road to Damascus was included in this opening statement.

> *Paul, an apostle—sent not from men nor by a man, but by Jesus Christ and God the Father, who raised him from the dead—and all the brothers and sisters with me (Galatians 1:1).*

Paul stated categorically that the Father raised Jesus from the dead. If there was any doubt about what Paul believed about Jesus, it has been clarified in the first sentence. In addition, he said the letter was from not just him, but also from the brothers and sisters who were with him.

> *To the churches in Galatia:*
> *Grace and peace to you from God our Father and the Lord Jesus Christ, who gave himself for our sins to rescue us from the present evil age, according to the will of our God and Father, to whom be glory for ever and ever. Amen*

(Galatians 1:2-5).

Every line is pregnant, not a word is wasted. Then Paul went straight to the point.

> *I am astonished that you are so quickly deserting the one who called you to live in the grace of Christ and are turning to a different gospel— which is really no gospel at all. Evidently some people are throwing you into confusion and are trying to pervert the gospel of Christ. But even if we or an angel from heaven should preach a gospel other than the one we preached to you, let them be under God's curse! As we have already said, so now I say again: If anybody is preaching to you a gospel other than what you accepted, let them be under God's curse (Galatians 1:6-8)!*

Evidently one of the accusations made against Paul was that he was a man pleaser trying to get man's approval. His opening remarks were clearly not meant to please people. Blunt and to the point, Paul believed this teaching by the Judaisers was another gospel and not the one received from Jesus.

He said any other gospel other than the one he preached was not the gospel at all, even if an angel preached it. He accused those who preached 'another gospel' of creating confusion and perverting the truth. These were strong words. The truth of the gospel is so important that to pervert or corrupt it has serious consequences. Paul invoked a curse on them not just once but twice. This language, which was unusual for twenty-first century readers, was an expression of the seriousness of the problem.

> *Am I now trying to win the approval of human beings, or of God? Or am I trying to please people? If I were still trying to please people, I would not be a servant of Christ (Galatians 1:10).*

In defending his gospel, Paul wrote,

> *For I want you know, brothers, that the gospel I preached is not something man made up. I did not receive it from any man, nor was I taught it, rather I received it by revelation of Jesus Christ (Galatians 1:11-12).*

It is important for Paul from the outset to make clear that the gospel came to him by revelation directly from Jesus. As an apostle appointed by Jesus, he spoke only what he heard from Jesus not from man. What he preached was directly from God and to challenge it or try to change it would bring them under the judgment of God.

One question that naturally arises is why did Paul need to communicate his gospel? Did they not know it? The answer is while they knew what Paul was teaching, hence the conflict, they did not understand his gospel nor why Paul taught what he did. Unlike the Twelve who received their gospel from John the Baptist and Jesus in his earthly ministry, Paul received his gospel directly from the risen Jesus.

In the following verses Paul outlined for them his life before his conversion and how God intervened and called him to preach. Then he talked about his call to be an apostle by Jesus.

> *But God who set me apart from birth and called me by his grace, was pleased to reveal his son in me so that I might preach him among the Gentiles I did not consult any man, nor did I go to Jerusalem to see those who were apostles before I was, but I went immediately to Arabia. Then after three years, I went up to Jerusalem to get acquainted with Cephas and stayed with him fifteen days. I saw none of the other apostles—only James, the Lord's brother. I assure you before God that what I am writing you is no lie (Galatians 1:15-20).*

CHAPTER XI

One of the accusations the Judaisers levelled against Paul was the source of his gospel was not apostolic, and because he was not taught by the Jerusalem apostles it was therefore unauthorised by the church in Jerusalem. His response was they were right. He was not taught by any man but by the Lord himself. This was Paul's trump card, and his gospel was indeed recognised and approved of by Jerusalem when he visited and also at the Council.

> *I presented to them the gospel that I preach among the Gentiles. I wanted to be sure I was not running and had not been running my race in vain (Galatians 2:2).*
>
> *They recognized that I had been entrusted with the task of preaching the gospel to the uncircumcised, just as Peter had been to the circumcised. For God, who was at work in Peter as an apostle to the circumcised, was also at work in me as an apostle to the Gentiles. James, Cephas and John, those esteemed as pillars, gave me and Barnabas the right hand of fellowship when they recognized the grace given to me. They agreed that we should go to the Gentiles, and they to the circumcised (Galatians 2:7-9).*

Paul, in defending his credentials as an apostle in this letter, cited the Jerusalem apostles' acceptance of his gospel teaching and told of his challenge to Peter to teach the true gospel.

In the Letter to the Galatians there is a recurring emphasis on Jerusalem and Judea. In Galatians 1-2 and 4, it is not difficult to conclude that the pharisaic troublemakers from Jerusalem and Judea kept going on into Syria, Cilicia, and Galatia after visiting Antioch.

Paul persistently struck at their home base and those Jerusalem pillars to whom they falsely appealed to for support of their position. This may also explain why Paul recounted the confrontation in Antioch that was so embarrassing to Peter and Barnabas in Galatians

2:11-21. His point was that the Judaisers' view had already been rejected at one of their prior stops, Antioch of Syria, the most prominent Gentile church. That rejection was public in scope, apostolic in authority involving both Peter and Paul, and apparently accepted as legitimate, otherwise Paul would not have appealed to it as authoritative for the Galatian situation.

After having described the events that had taken place, Paul laid out before his readers the truth of the gospel he preached.

> *We who are Jews by birth and not sinful Gentiles know that a person is not justified by the works of the law, but by the faith of Jesus Christ. So we, too, have put our faith in Christ Jesus that we may be justified by the faithfulness of Christ and not by the works of the law, because by the works of the law no one will be justified. But if, in seeking to be justified by Christ, we Jews find ourselves also among the sinners, doesn't that mean that Christ promotes sin? Absolutely not! If I rebuild what I destroyed, then I really would be a lawbreaker.*
>
> *For through the law I died to the law so that I might live for God. I have been crucified with Christ and I no longer live, but Christ lives in me. The life I now live in the body, I live by the faith of the Son of God, who loved me and gave himself for me. I do not set aside the grace of God, for if righteousness could be gained through the law, Christ died for nothing! (Galatians 2:15-21)*

This is a crucial passage that explains how Paul saw and understood the gospel. It is so important I want to pause here and reflect on it. When Paul wrote this letter, he wrote it in Greek, the language that most people spoke and understood at that time. We, however, do not speak Greek and need to have it translated into

CHAPTER XI

our own languages. Throughout this book I have consistently used the New International Version (NIV) translation. It is important to remember that this translation, whilst it tries to be as close a translation of the original Greek as it can be, it is nonetheless, to some level, an interpretation by the translators and may reflect the translators theological bias and understanding. This is never more true than in this passage.

There are several little words in the passage that need to be very carefully translated to reflect the original intent and message that Paul communicated to the Galatians. The overriding message is that we can do nothing ourselves to bring about our own salvation. It has all been done and accomplished by the work of Jesus on the cross. When Paul wrote, "(we) know that a person is not justified by the works of the law, but by the faith of Jesus Christ," in Galatians 2:16, he was saying we are not justified or made righteous by works of the law. Rather, we are justified by the faith of Jesus Christ. It is Jesus' faith that brings about our justification. But the translators of the NIV translated this sentence to read, "a person is not justified by the works of the law, but by faith in Jesus Christ." The sense is completely opposite when translated as 'faith in Jesus' rather than the 'faith of Jesus'. It is suggesting that we have to have faith in Jesus to receive justification.

This has led to the belief that we may not be justified if our faith in Jesus is not strong enough or is inadequate. We are equally in danger of self-righteousness if we think our faith is sufficient. It is subtle, but it is like the words of the Pharisees or Judaisers who were inserting circumcision as a requirement for salvation. Even faith, if it is our faith that leads to salvation takes away the work of the cross. Paul made clear it was what Jesus has done. This was fundamental for Paul. He would be appalled at the inference that this simple translation error has led to.

To follow the argument that Paul made in Galatians 2:16,

> "*So we, too, have put our faith in Christ Jesus that we may be justified by the faith of Christ and not by the works of the law.*"

He was saying we put our faith in Christ Jesus, that is, we believe what he says and has done is true and then we are justified and made right with God because of the faithfulness of Jesus.

The same applies to one of the first verses I was encouraged to memorise after becoming a Christian, the oft quoted verse Galatians 2:20. I always felt condemned by it because I felt my faith was never strong enough to live the Christian life,

> "*I have been crucified with Christ and I no longer live, but Christ lives in me. The life I now live in the body, I live by faith in the Son of God, who loved me and gave himself for me.*"

When I saw that it was the faithfulness of Jesus at work in me that enabled me to live the Christian life rather than my efforts to have sufficient faith in Jesus, it changed everything. There was joy and freedom in this, not striving and condemnation.

> "*I have been crucified with Christ and I no longer live, but Christ lives in me. The life I now live in the body, I live by faith of the Son of God, who loved me and gave himself for me.*"

Paul's gospel is a gospel of freedom and receiving the grace of the Lord Jesus that he freely gives to us. His faithfulness brings about our salvation.

In Galatians Chapter 3, Paul changed tracks slightly.

When Paul wrote this letter to the Galatians, he of course did not divide it up into chapters and verses. The process of dividing

CHAPTER XI

the Bible into chapters and verses began in the twelfth century when chapters were inserted. In 1551, Robert Estienne added verse divisions to his edition of the New Testament. This was all designed to help readers find their favourite bits of the Bible with ease. Then in 1556, the Geneva Bible added them, and the rest is history.

Thus, moving into Chapter 3 is not the start of a new part of the letter, it is rather a continuation and further elaboration of Paul's thinking.

He was speaking directly to people in Galatia, many of whom he would have known personally, and his frustration boiled over.

"You foolish Galatians! Who has bewitched you? Before your very eyes Jesus Christ was clearly portrayed as crucified. I would like to learn just one thing from you: Did you receive the Spirit by the works of the law, or by believing what you heard? Are you so foolish? After beginning by means of the Spirit, are you now trying to finish by means of the flesh? Have you experienced so much in vain—if it really was in vain? So again I ask, does God give you his Spirit and work miracles among you by the works of the law, or by your believing what you heard" (Galatians 3:1-5).

Paul was not being offensive when he called them foolish, he was exercising tough love. He loved them, but he could not abide what happened to them. He concluded that they had been "bewitched". This was a strong word to use.

In English, the clue is easily recognised in the word. The word speaks of witchcraft, entrapment and malign activity by Satan. This was absolutely the right word to use because the origin of this teaching forced them to try to get right with God through their own effort, their own self-righteousness, through their own futile attempts. Going back to the Garden of Eden and the fruit of the Tree of the Knowledge of Good and Evil and Satan's corrupt wisdom, to keep the rules and obey the law is satanic in origin. What the Galatians were being told to do was to essentially eat from the fruit of the wrong tree rather than the Tree of Life.

Paul highlighted the result in their lives of his presentation of the gospel by asking a simple and obvious question, did they receive the Spirit by the works of the law or by believing what they heard? Their introduction to the good news that Paul brought was accompanied by miracles and the anointing of the Holy Spirit on them.

Paul continued the argument calling Abraham into the discussion. He cites Abraham's faith and how it was credited to him as righteousness (Gal. 3:6). He then went on to show that those who have this gift of faith are the children and spiritual descendants of Abraham and this included believing Gentiles too. "All nations will be blessed through you." So those who rely on faith are blessed along with Abraham, the man of faith (Gal. 3:9). In contrast, Paul wrote those who rely on the works of the law are under a curse, as it is written: "Cursed is everyone who does not continue to do everything written in the Book of the Law" (Deuteronomy 27:26). Paul drew on his own deep, extensive knowledge of Old Testament scripture. He was, in some ways, beating the Judaisers at their own game. Paul continued,

> *"Clearly no one who relies on the law is justified before God, because "the righteous will live by faith." The law is not based on faith; on the contrary, it says, "The person who does these things will live by them." Christ redeemed us from the curse of the law by becoming a curse for us, for it is written: "Cursed is everyone who is hung on a tree" (Galatians 3:11-13).*

CHAPTER XI

Paul then explained what Jesus has done for us. He received this by revelation from Jesus himself.

'He redeemed us in order that the blessing given to Abraham might come to the Gentiles through Christ Jesus, so that by faith we might receive the promise of the Spirit' (Galatians 3:14).

The use of the word redeemed is important as Paul's explanation unfolds in the next part of the letter. What Jesus has done in redeeming us has a significant impact on how we understand what Paul wrote. The teaching on redemption has its roots in the Old Testament, but in the New Testament it is almost exclusively used by Paul. Redemption is the act of buying something back or paying a price or ransom to return something to your possession. Redemption is the English translation of the Greek word *'agorazo'*, meaning "to purchase in the marketplace." In ancient times, it often referred to the act of buying a slave. It carried the meaning of freeing someone from chains, prison, or slavery. Paul used the word four times, twice in Galatians 3:13 and 4:5, then in Ephesians 5:16 and Colossians 4:5. Redemption always involves going from something to something else. In this case, it is Christ freeing us from the bondage of the law to freedom of a new life in him.

The other Greek word connected with redemption is 'lutroo', meaning "to obtain release by the payment of a price. The price, or ransom, in Christianity was Christ's precious blood obtaining our release from sin and death. It is used ten times in the New Testament, seven of which are by Paul. In Romans 3:24, Paul expanded what he had first written in Galatians.

There is no difference between Jew and Gentile, for all have sinned and fall short of the glory of God, and all are justified freely by his grace through the redemption that came by Christ Jesus (Romans 3:22-24).

The most important issue in redemption and Paul's use of the word is that it describes the process of salvation. It brings together the two strains in redemption and being redeemed. Something that was once owned or possessed but has been lost is bought back. A price has been paid in order to get it back into its original owner's possession. The process is completely the initiative of God the Father in redeeming his wayward and lost children. God does this by sending his son Jesus to redeem us, that is buy back that which belonged to him in the first place. In Paul's teaching, he recognised by revelation that we were God the Father's creation and offspring in the first instance.

Much of what Paul wrote about in Galatians, he amplified and expounded upon in other letters. As is the case in Ephesians chapter 1 where he wrote,

> *"Praise be to the God and Father of our Lord Jesus Christ, who has blessed us in the heavenly realms with every spiritual blessing in Christ. For he chose us in him before the creation of the world to be holy and blameless in his sight. In love he predestined us to be placed as sons through Jesus Christ, in accordance with his pleasure and will— to the praise of his glorious grace, which he has freely given us in the One he loves. In him we have redemption through his blood, the forgiveness of sin, in accordance with the riches of God's grace that he lavished on us with all wisdom and understanding" (Ephesians 1:3-8).*

Redemption is in the background of the rest of Chapter 4 of Galatians. Before getting there, Paul took another look at the Law. This had been a focus of the Judaisers, so Paul looked at what the point of the law was in the first place. Again, he later expounded

CHAPTER XI

on this in Romans Chapter 7.

In Galatians, he continued by writing that the covenants based on law could not be changed. Promises spoken to Abraham and his Seed, that is Jesus, still stand. The law of Moses given 430 years later does not set aside the covenant or promise given to Abraham. Paul asked a series of obvious questions. Why, then, was the law given at all? Is the law opposed to the promises of God? His answer was that the law was given because of man's sin and was in place until the 'Seed', that is Jesus, to whom the promise referred had come. For if the Law of Moses could have imparted life, then righteousness would certainly have come by the law. But the Law kept everything locked up under the control of sin so that what was promised, being given through the faith of Jesus Christ, might be given to those who believe. Note again the difference 'in' and 'of' makes in relation to this last phrase in Galatians 3:22.

Paul also wrote about the coming of faith in Galatians 3:23, saying that we were held in custody under the law, locked up until the faith that was to come would be revealed. The faith he wrote of is Jesus and his faithfulness and commitment to being obedient to his Father. His willingness to suffer and die on the cross and by the shedding of his blood to bring redemption and reconciliation. Some modern translators have not been clear enough, confusing whose faith Paul spoke of. Paul wrote about the faith of Jesus not our faith in Jesus.

CHAPTER XII

THE SON AND HEIR.

*P*aul walked up and down the room as thoughts and inspiration tumbled out of his heart and mouth. Many times, Tychicus had to ask him to slow down and repeat what he said. Tychicus was having trouble seeing the parchment as the light of the lamp became poor.

"Paul," he finally said, "we have to stop. I can barely see the page. It's not good for my eyes, let alone yours."

"Yes, of course, my son. I did not mean to push you. It's just so important that we get this down and sent off as soon as we can," Paul answered.

Feeling like a father to the young scribe who was now his amanuensis or secretarial assistant, Paul had taken to calling Tychicus 'my son'. He wondered about that. Tychicus was a very important part of his emerging team. He would write down a number of Paul's letters in the future as Paul dictated them.

"How long have you been an amanuensis, Tychicus?" asked Paul.

"Oh, quite a few years now. When I first became a slave, they realised I could read and write. Our family was quite well off and my father had us children educated in our home. When he died suddenly, creditors took our home, and we were all sold as slaves. It was terrible. I was born a freeman. Becoming a slave at twelve years old was devastating. The man who bought me took me into his home and I was tasked to work in the nursery looking after his children, a boy and a girl. Because I

CHAPTER XII

could read and write, I was soon given the task of being a pedagogue. Amongst other things, whenever they went out, I went along as their guardian. As I got older, I became their tutor and was responsible for most of their education. The family was good to me and kind, even though I was a slave. Then the day came when the father, my master, said it was time to recognise his son as his official heir. We got the boy ready and off we went to the forum for the ceremony. You know what happens don't you?"

"Yes," said Paul. "Barnabas and I were guests of the Proconsul of Cyprus, Sergius Paulus when he recognised his son."

"Well, after that my job was more or less done. I thought I might end up being sold again, but to my amazement my master decided to give me my freedom. He said it was in gratitude for all my work as a tutor and guardian of his son. I was set free and given my certificate of manumission that shows I am a free man. That is how I ended up here in Antioch." Tychicus paused thoughtfully.

"That is why, Paul, what you are teaching is so important to me. I never want to be a slave again, either in this world or in the spiritual world. I am not going back to that old way of life. I am tired of keeping those rules, working my head off. It just wore me out."

Paul was lost in thought. "Tomorrow then. As soon as it is light, we will continue. You have given me much to think about, my son."

∿∧∿∧∿

Paul began to write again but he was seeing things he had only had glimpses of before. Revelation after revelation filled his heart. Things that Jesus had been saying to him over many years were now all coming together as he wrote to the Galatians. The language of the nursery and the place of the pedagogues or guardians and trustees who looked after the children filled his heart. He saw that the child, even though one day he would be the heir was virtually like a slave. The Law of Moses had been like these guardians, like a schoolmaster, but when Jesus came all that changed. We became recognised by God the Father as his sons and daughters because of the faithfulness of Jesus.

> *"So the law was our guardian until Christ came that we might be justified by faith. Now that this faith has come, we are no longer under a guardian. Instead you are all sons of God through the faith of Christ Jesus, for all of you who were baptized into Christ have clothed yourselves with Christ. There is neither Jew nor Gentile, neither slave nor free, there is neither male and nor female, for you are all one in Christ Jesus. If you belong to Christ, then you are Abraham's seed, and heirs according to the promise."* (Galatians 3:24-29).

Here was the simple answer to the Judaisers. As he wrote, more revelation came to him. Paul saw that the process of bringing us into sonship was redemption through the death of Jesus for us on the cross. The result of redemption was that we are re-placed in our true status as sons because we are heirs. Sonship is all about receiving the gift that the Father has given us.

God the Father of the Lord Jesus was central to Paul's thinking and as Christians, we are brought into a relationship with God as Father through the faith of Christ. Paul described what it is like to live as sons and daughters and introduced the whole revelation of sonship. All people who are baptized into Christ are one and are God's sons, Abraham's offspring and heirs to God's promise.

When Paul talked about being baptised into Christ, he no doubt thought about his own baptism in Damascus many years before.

CHAPTER XII

There was a sense of washing and cleansing of his sinful life that Jesus had dealt with by the shedding of his blood on the cross. Baptism for Paul was rich with symbolism. It was like a burial of his old life and being raised to a new life in Christ as he would later write in Colossians. But also, like at Jesus' own baptism, it is a time or declaration by the Father that he too was his beloved son and he was proud of him.

Paul shared with the Galatians, and subsequently all of us, the dramatic climax of this revelation.

> *"What I am saying is that as long as an heir is underage, he is no different from a slave, although he owns the whole estate. The heir is subject to guardians and trustees until the time set by his father. So also, when we were underage, we were in slavery under the elemental spiritual forces of the world. But when the set time had fully come, God sent his Son, born of a woman, born under the law, to redeem those under the law, that we might receive the full rights of sons. Because you are his sons, God sent the Spirit of his Son into our hearts, the Spirit who calls out, "Abba, Father." So you are no longer a slave, but God's child; and since you are his child, God has made you also an heir"* (Galatians 4:1-7).

Paul introduced this in verses 1 and 2 by referring to a ceremony known as 'Son Placing". He must have witnessed this at some point as I creatively recounted during his visit to Cyprus in the fictional narrative at the beginning of Chapter 8 in this book. There is no biblical hint of such an event happening, but I added the scene purely to give a visual context to this ceremony that Paul referred to in Galatians 4:1-2.

This ceremony of 'son placing', of recognising a son and heir by a father was referred to in Greek as 'huiothesia', which Paul introduced us to in Galatians 4:5. I translate it in this passage along with the NIV as a phrase, *"receive the full rights of sons"*. He used this word five times in his letters (Galatians 4:5; Romans 8:15,23; Romans 9:4; Ephesians 1:5), and it has proven difficult to translate. It is a compound word made up of two Greek words, 'huios' which means 'son' and 'thesia' which means 'placing' from the verb 'to place'.

Huiothesia describes a ceremony that occurred within the Roman culture in which a male child of a citizen achieved the status of manhood and was officially recognised as the son and heir by his father, the paterfamilias. Prior to the ceremony, a son was considered to have the status of a slave in his father's house, even though he had the potential to inherit his father's wealth (The Story of Civilization, Vol. 3: Caesar and Christ, 1972, p. 57). The 'son placing ceremony' occurred sometime in a boy's teenage years when his father determined it was time for him to pass from being a child under the absolute power of his father into adulthood and his true status as son and heir.

In this public ceremony, the young man would remove the toga he wore as a boy and put on the *'toga virilis'*, the toga of manhood. This ceremony marked his entry into full citizenship in the empire and the right to vote in the assembly. Not only this, but also after the 'son placing ceremony', the son became fully legally invested with all of the rights, powers, and privileges of being a son and heir to his father's possessions, wealth, and status. No longer was he viewed as a child, he was a fully participating member of his society and family (Harrill, 2002; Fraschetti, 1997; *"Roman Children,"* Classics Unveiled.com).

Apparently, when the father publicly introduced his designated son and heir, he announced this by declaring this boy was his son whom

CHAPTER XII

he loved and of whom he was proud. This would have resonated with Paul as these were the words God the Father spoke over Jesus at his baptism by John in the River Jordan. The father would then place the toga on his heir along with a ring of authority on his finger. The story known as 'The Prodigal Son' told by Jesus in Luke 15 has the same imagery. The returning son is clothed in the best robe and a ring is placed on his finger denoting his status again as a son.

It should be noted that the one who was 'placed as a son' was generally already the biological child of the father, thus it was not an adoption into the father's household.

However, within Roman and Greek culture, many times there was not a male son to appoint as an heir. Infant mortality was high, and many children did not reach adulthood. To overcome this difficulty, the Romans, introduced the idea of adoption. They called it 'adoptio filio'. This allowed a Roman father to adopt a boy and go through the son placing ceremony with the adopted boy. These adoptions were not necessarily of orphans. Many times, they were spare sons, that is, sons of a man who had more than one. He could effectively sell a son to a friend or colleague who was childless. This practice was seen many times in the imperial family where murder and assassination were tragically very common. The reigning emperor would adopt and appoint new heirs after the last one died.

By the fourth century AD, the church in the west was predominantly Latin speaking and had as much trouble reading the Greek New Testament, as we do. There were a number of poor Latin versions of the bible circulating. Around 400 AD, Jerome, a Roman scholar and monk undertook the task of producing a translation of the whole Bible from Greek and Hebrew. This was referred to as the Vulgate and was the accepted translation used by the Roman Catholic Church right into the twentieth century. When Jerome encountered this Greek word 'huiothesia', he chose to translate this word in Latin as 'adoptio'. Like a number of Jerome's translations in the Vulgate, it leaves a lot to be desired. Consequently, adoption became a common translation of this word.

In 1382, when John Wycliffe produced his first translation of the Bible into English, he translated from Jerome's Latin Vulgate. Thus, when he came to this word, he translated it into English as 'adoption'. The idea of adoption was still understood and practiced, but the 'son placing ceremony' of the ancient world was long gone from conscious memory.

In the Reformation of the sixteenth century when the Bible was being translated into many European languages, the translators encountered this word and had to decide how to translate it. In the English-speaking world, the first serious translation of the New Testament from Greek was undertaken in 1530 by William Tyndale who had a very clear understanding of the Fatherhood of God and how he recognises us as sons. In his translation, he tried to avoid the word adoption. In Galatians 4, Tyndale translates, *"we through election might receive the inheritance that belongeth unto the natural sons."*[1] However, his translation was not accepted, and he was burnt as a heretic in Brussels in 1536. Considering Tyndale's translations rather cumbersome, when the 1611 authorised King James Version of the Bible was published, all five references had retreated into adoption.

It is only in recent years that the English-speaking world has revisited this translation. It is notable that NT Wright in his commentaries translates 'huiothesia' as 'sonship.'

In Northern European languages, they follow Luther's translation which does not carry the idea of adoption at all. In the Latin-based languages such as Spanish and especially French, which follows

CHAPTER XII

Calvin's teaching, they have gone for adoption.

In the New Testament itself, only Paul used this word. What did Paul mean when used this word? Paul's original imagery of 'huiothesia', literally "placing as a son" as opposed to being adopted within God's kingdom profoundly affects our relationship with God. Adoption as applied to our relationship with God is problematic as it changes our fundamental status as God's offspring. When a child is adopted into a family, he remains physically the same person. No change of name or falsification of birth records will ever eliminate the biological reality. The child is still the offspring of his natural parents. That child's DNA will always remain different, separate, and unrelated to his adoptive parents.

However, Paul taught that we are God's offspring, created in his image, especially as we consider that he was the Father of Adam and Eve. Paul used this argument in Acts 17:28-29 when talking to Greeks in Athens on his second missionary journey. Luke, in the genealogy of Jesus, traces the family line of Jesus through his mother back to Adam who is described as a son of God (Luke 3:38). As their descendants, our own DNA carries the fingerprints of divine origins. God even tells us that he is intimately involved with the physical creation of each one of us. He 'knits' us together in our mother's womb, according to Psalm 139:13-16. This is because God is our real Father.

When we are born, we essentially become slaves of the fallen world of men that we are born into. However, this does not change our status as God's offspring. We are still his children. We are just separated from intimate relationship with him because of our sin. The gospel that Paul preached is about a loving Father who provided a way for us to be reconciled to him, to have those chains of slavery broken. Paul said this is through the blood of Jesus, God's son, shed for us on the cross. The act of becoming a follower of Jesus allows us to begin the process of redemption. 'Huiothesia' is the result of this process. We become a full and participatory member of the Father's family, with full rights as his children. God the Father does not do adoption. He restores things to their proper order and place in his family.

By Paul's use of this word in Galatians 4:5, it is obvious that the English word 'adoption' does not fit the context, whereas 'sonship' or 'receiving the rights of a son', or something like it is precisely what Paul spoke of. The sons who have not yet come of age do not need to be adopted because they were sons already. But they do need to come into a situation in which they can exercise their full rights as sons. Paul made clear his main concerns:

"As proof that you are sons, God sent the spirit of his Son into our hearts, crying out 'Abba, Father!' So you are no longer a slave, but God's child; and since you are his child, God has made you also an heir" (Galatians 4:6-7).

The translation of 'huiothesia' as adoption does not convey the meaning that Paul intended. Yet many eminent and famous theologians and Christian leaders have written whole books about adoption. The premise is that God adopts us into his family. The English word adoption refers to a legal process by which a person who wants to have a child can legally recognise and adopt a child who is not biologically their own. Thus, the child will be officially recognised as their own, and consequently have the same legal status as any other children they may have. At first glance, this seems to fit what God has done, but the premise is wrong. There are a number of reasons why adoption is not the proper English word to convey Paul's meaning in the passages where he used 'huiothesia'.

In English, adoption means the child who is adopted is not

CHAPTER XII

a person's child in any sense before the adoption took place. This meaning conflicts with the way Paul used 'huiothesia' in Galatians 4:5.

Secondly, adoption in English refers primarily to the legal contract that makes a person one's child, whereas in Paul's use of 'huiothesia', this is the end result of redemption. Redemption is the process by which God the Father reconciles us to himself and brings us into a position of sons in relationship with the Father.

Equally significant, there is a serious emotional and psychological problem with using the word adoption. Many children who have been adopted are troubled about the fact that they are adopted. They may be very comfortable that their adoptive parents wanted them and were happy to adopt them. However, they often wonder who their birth parents were. Why did they not want to keep them? Many then try to seek out and locate their biological mother or father. In some cases, these kinds of thoughts can result in children suspecting there must have been something wrong with them or that their birth parents did not want them and then gave them up. It is obvious that any thoughts of this kind are completely out of place in the contexts where Paul used 'huiothesia'.

In the situation Paul referred to, there are no other parents who have given up the children first so that God can adopt them. Indeed, in Acts 17:28 when addressing a Greek audience, Paul declared we have always been God's offspring. God has always been our Father and we have always been his offspring, but we have lost the relationship because of the fall and our sin. He sent Jesus into the world to reveal that he is and always was Father and that through the faith of Christ and his redeeming work on the cross, we are brought home to receive back our status as sons.

As Paul used the term 'huiothesia', the meaning refers to the status of being a son. In particular, two facts result from that status.

THE SON AND HEIR

First, we recognise ourselves to be God's child, and therefore we feel it is right to address God as "Father." Paul connected this very strongly with the receiving of the Spirit of God in Galatians 4:6. He also picked this up in Romans 8:15-16 and Ephesians 1:13. Secondly, there is the fact that all of the promises God has made to his people are made especially to us as his sons. As God's sons, we can expect to receive everything God has promised his people. Paul introduced the idea that we are God's 'heirs' in Galatians 4:7 and also in Romans 8:17-25 and Ephesians 1:3-14.

Through his faithfulness, we are then placed in a position of sons or as Paul said, we receive from the Holy Spirit, the Father's gift of sonship.

It cannot be overstated that this first letter of Paul is of immense significance in setting out the doctrine of the revelation of God as a Father who redeems us and puts us in place as his sons. The doctrine of sonship is central to understanding the rest of the New Testament and God's dealings with mankind.

∿∿∿

With all of these foundational truths in place, Paul turned in the letter to address a number of practical implications that arise. He spoke directly to them as his brothers and sisters. Much of what he wrote contrasted being slaves and freemen. He had already told them their sonship meant there is no distinction between being a Jew or Greek, man or woman or even slave or free. They are all united and one in Christ (Gal.3:23). He drew this out in more practical detail.

Formerly, when you did not know God, you were slaves to those who by nature are not gods. But now that you know God or rather are known by God, how is it that you

CHAPTER XII

are turning back to those weak and miserable forces? Do you wish to be enslaved by them all over again? You are observing special days and months and seasons and years! I fear for you, that somehow I have wasted my efforts on you (Galatians 4:8-11).

Paul became extremely personal with them reminding them of the depth of their relationship with him.

I plead with you, brothers and sisters, become like me, for I became like you. You did me no wrong. As you know, it was because of an illness that I first preached the gospel to you, and even though my illness was a trial to you, you did not treat me with contempt or scorn. Instead, you welcomed me as if I were an angel of God, as if I were Christ Jesus himself. Where, then, is your blessing of me now? I can testify that, if you could have done so, you would have torn out your eyes and given them to me. Have I now become your enemy by telling you the truth? (Galatians 4:12-16)

Then he turned his attention to those who have caused so much trouble.

Those people are zealous to win you over, but for no good. What they want is to alienate you from us, so that you may have zeal for them. It is fine to be zealous, provided the purpose is good, and to be so always, not just when I am with you. My dear children, for whom I am again in the pains of childbirth until Christ is formed in you, how I wish I could be with you now and change my tone, because I am perplexed about you! (Galatians 4:17-22)

He showed them what slavery looked like if they went back by drawing on the story of Abraham and Sarah and the slave girl Hagar.

His reference to this story suggested this may have been one of the so called biblical arguments used by the Judaisers. Paul urged them to recognise that through being in Christ they are children of promise and not children of the slave girl.

> *Now you, brothers and sisters, like Isaac, are children of promise. At that time the son born according to the flesh persecuted the son born by the power of the Spirit. It is the same now. But what does Scripture say? "Get rid of the slave woman and her son, for the slave woman's son will never share in the inheritance with the free woman's son." Therefore, brothers and sisters, we are not children of the slave woman, but of the free woman. It is for freedom that Christ has set us free. Stand firm, then, and do not let yourselves be burdened again by a yoke of slavery (Galatians 4:28-5:1).*

In the next section of the letter, Paul continued to contrast for them the difference between being sons who are free in Christ and the slavery the Judaisers would force them back into, warning them that being circumcised would put them into a serious place of obligation to obey all the details of the law.

> *"Mark my words! I, Paul, tell you that if you let yourselves be circumcised, Christ will be of no value to you at all. Again I declare to every man who lets himself be circumcised that he is obligated to obey the whole law" (Galatians 5:2-3).*

Paul wrote this attempt to be justified by the law would alienate them from Jesus and amounts to falling away completely from grace. Their life in the Spirit however brings righteousness and hope. Because they are in Christ neither circumcision nor uncircumcision has any value. The only thing that counts is faith expressing itself

CHAPTER XII

through love.

Paul's passion is evident as he poured out his concern for them. His natural anger at those who have misled them rose as he saw the confusion they have created. Tychicus probably had to slow him down once more.

> *"You were running a good race. Who cut in on you to keep you from obeying the truth? That kind of persuasion does not come from the one who calls you. "A little yeast works through the whole batch of dough." I am confident in the Lord that you will take no other view. The one who is throwing you into confusion, whoever that may be, will have to pay the penalty. Brothers and sisters, if I am still preaching circumcision, why am I still being persecuted? In that case the offence of the cross has been abolished. As for those agitators, I wish they would go the whole way and emasculate themselves (Galatians 5:7-12).*

Paul was not advocating freedom as a way of indulging the flesh rather to live the life of love by walking in the Spirit. Paul said life in Christ is living a life of love for one another. In his letter to the Romans in chapters 7, he explored this issue of the relationship of the Law of Moses and the law of sin and death at work in us. Then, magnificently in chapter 8 of Romans, he showed how we as sons live in a new law, a third law which is the law of the Spirit of life in Christ Jesus that sets us free from the laws of sin and death. James Jordan explores this revelation in greater detail in his book, *The Ancient Road Rediscovered* in a chapter entitled 'The Third Law',

Paul pointed out that the trouble in their churches had resulted in accusations against each other and all manner of personal attacks. This is so typical of what happens when we live from the wrong tree, the Tree of the Knowledge of Good and Evil. In our desire to say who is right and who is wrong, we become judgmental of each other. This has led to centuries of tragedy in the history of the Church when people who were deemed wrong were dragged out and tortured and burned to death.

> *"You, my brothers and sisters, were called to be free. But do not use your freedom to indulge the flesh; rather, serve one another humbly in love. For the entire law is fulfilled in keeping this one command: "Love your neighbour as yourself." If you bite and devour each other, watch out or you will be destroyed by each other.*
>
> *So I say, walk by the Spirit, and you will not gratify the desires of the flesh. For the flesh desires what is contrary to the Spirit, and the Spirit what is contrary to the flesh. They are in conflict with each other, so that you are not to do whatever you want. But if you are led by the Spirit, you are not under the law.*
>
> *The acts of the flesh are obvious: sexual immorality, impurity and debauchery; idolatry and witchcraft; hatred, discord, jealousy, fits of rage, selfish ambition, dissensions, factions and envy; drunkenness, orgies, and the like. I warn you, as I did before, that those who live like this will not inherit the kingdom of God.*
>
> *But the fruit of the Spirit is love, joy, peace, forbearance, kindness, goodness, faithfulness, gentleness and self-control. Against such things there is no law. Those who belong to Christ Jesus have crucified the flesh with its passions and desires. Since we live by the Spirit, let us keep in step with the Spirit. Let us not become conceited, provoking and envying each other"* (Galatians 5:13-25).

In the final part of the letter to the Galatians, Paul became intensely practical addressing an issue that had been reported to him in some way. It involved what to do about a person who is caught in sin after having become a Christian and being 'in Christ.' He showed how the law of Love operates in situations like this. In dealing with the person who has fallen, the goal is gentle restoration and mutual accountability. It involves carrying each other's burdens whilst recognising individual responsibility. There are times when the fallen brother needs to be carried by the loving community of those who are in Christ. I have explored these issues in my book, *Falling from grace into Grace and being caught by the Father* (2013).

> *"Brothers and sisters, if someone is caught in a sin, you who live by the Spirit should restore that person gently. But watch yourselves, or you also may be tempted. Carry each other's burdens, and in this way you will fulfil the law of Christ. If anyone thinks they are something when they are not, they deceive themselves. Each one should test their own actions. Then they can take pride in themselves alone, without comparing themselves to someone else, for each one should carry their own load. Nevertheless, the one who receives instruction in the word should share all good things with their instructor.*
>
> *Do not be deceived: God cannot be mocked. A man reaps what he sows. Whoever sows to please their flesh, from the flesh will reap destruction; whoever sows to please the Spirit, from the Spirit will reap eternal life. Let us not become weary in doing good, for at the proper time we will reap a harvest if we do not give up. Therefore, as we have opportunity, let us do good to all people, especially to those who belong to the family of believers (Galatians 6:1-10).*

As Paul drew to the end of the letter, it was as if he took the stylus from Tychicus' hand and wrote the lines himself.

> *"See what large letters I use as I write to you with my own hand!"*

Regarding this conclusion, Bishop Lightfoot, says in his commentary on Galatians: "At this point the apostle takes the pen from his amanuensis and the concluding paragraph is written with his own hand. He writes a whole paragraph, summing up the main lessons of the epistle in terse, eager, disjointed sentences. He writes it, too, in large, bold characters that his hand-writing may reflect the energy and determination of his soul."

He urged them in one last warning not to give in to being compelled to be circumcised.

> *"Those who want to impress people by means of the flesh are trying to compel you to be circumcised. The only reason they do this is to avoid being persecuted for the cross of Christ. Not even those who are circumcised keep the law, yet they want you to be circumcised that they may boast about your circumcision in the flesh. May I never boast except in the cross of our Lord Jesus Christ, through which the world has been crucified to me, and I to the world. Neither circumcision nor uncircumcision means anything; what counts is the new creation.*
>
> *Peace and mercy to all who follow this rule, to the Israel of God. From now on, let no one cause me trouble, for I bear on my body the marks of Jesus.*

CHAPTER XII

The grace of our Lord Jesus Christ be with your spirit, brothers and sisters.
Amen" (Galatians 6:12-18).

Finally, Paul stopped and put the pen down, handing it back to Tychicus. He doesn't say that Tychicus was the scribe. I have assumed that he was as he was in other letters of Paul. It does not really matter. This letter was the culmination of years of receiving revelation from Jesus, and Paul shared it with the Galatians and all his readers.

In the coming years, as his life continued, Paul would dig deeper into these truths and would write more about them in his other letters. But the foundation stone has been laid. The glorious truth he had seen that we are in Christ and as a result are sons and daughters of God our Father is a cornerstone of the Christian faith.

EPILOGUE

Paul dispatched the letter to the Galatians and sometime later, he decided to visit them personally, embarking on his second missionary journey. This time, he took Silas with him rather than Barnabas. Luke recounts these stories for us in Acts. In Lystra, Paul connected with Timothy who I imagined had alerted him to the events in Galatia. There was no evidence that it was Timothy, but someone did. In response to a vision, Paul moved on and went on to Macedonia on the European mainland. At this point, doctor Luke joined the team, and Paul had his doctor with him at last. Luke recounts these journeys and the triumphs and trials they faced until Paul ends up where we began this story in Caesarea with him in prison waiting to be tried and eventually sent to Rome.

Luke tells us all about the eventful journey and the shipwreck in the shores of the Mediterranean Island of Malta and his eventual arrival in Rome.

Apparently, Mark was with Paul during his first imprisonment in Rome when Paul wrote the four prison epistles: Ephesians, Philippians Colossians, and Philemon. Paul instructed the trusted Tychicus to carry the letters to the receivers in the city of Colosse and Ephesus.

EPILOGUE

There is evidence of another missionary journey by Paul after the end of Acts possibly between AD 62-67, where he is last seen under house arrest in Rome in Acts 28. The evidence comes from Paul's own letters. According to Romans 15:24,28, Paul's intention was to visit Spain. In the fourth century, Eusebius implies that Paul was released after his first Roman imprisonment. There are statements in early Christian literature that say he took the gospel to Spain. Paul also mentioned places visited in his letters not recorded in Acts.

At some point, he returned to Rome and was imprisoned again. Perhaps he was caught up like Peter, who was supposedly crucified outside the city on a hill on the north bank of the River Tiber, in the violent attack launched on Christians in the city during the reign of the emperor Nero. In 67 AD, Nero made Christians the scapegoat for the burning of a major part of the city of Rome that he wanted to build his new palace on.

It is believed that Paul was beheaded in Rome during this brief but violent outbreak of persecution. As a Roman citizen, he was spared crucifixion. The church of San Paolo Fuori i Muri in Rome is supposedly built over his tomb. This is also outside the ancient walls of Rome to the south west.

The last words Paul wrote in his second letter to Timothy reflect the impending crisis and his martyrdom. All his Christian life, he had been a witness now he would bear witness in the ultimate way by laying down his life for the gospel.

I take my leave at this point and give the last words to Paul. They are from the second letter he wrote to his son in the faith Timothy, chapter 4 verses 6-13.

> *"For I am already being poured out like a drink offering, and the time for my departure is near. I have fought the good fight, I have finished the race, I have kept the faith.*

EPILOGUE

Now there is in store for me the crown of righteousness, which the Lord, the righteous Judge, will award to me on that day—and not only to me, but also to all who have longed for his appearing.
Do your best to come to me quickly, for Demas, because he loved this world, has deserted me and has gone to Thessalonica. Crescens has gone to Galatia, and Titus to Dalmatia. Only Luke is with me. Get Mark and bring him with you, because he is helpful to me in my ministry. I sent Tychicus to Ephesus. When you come, bring the cloak that I left with Carpus at Troas, and my scrolls, especially the parchments.
Alexander the metalworker did me a great deal of harm. The Lord will repay him for what he has done. You too should be on your guard against him, because he strongly opposed our message. At my first defense, no one came to my support, but everyone deserted me. May it not be held against them. But the Lord stood at my side and gave me strength, so that through me the message might be fully proclaimed and all the Gentiles might hear it. And I was delivered from the lion's mouth. The Lord will rescue me from every evil attack and will bring me safely to his heavenly kingdom. To him be glory for ever and ever. Amen.
Greet Priscilla and Aquila and the household of Onesiphorus. Erastus stayed in Corinth, and I left Trophimus sick in Miletus. Do your best to get here before winter. Eubulus greets you, and so do Pudens, Linus, Claudia and all the brothers and sisters.
The Lord be with your spirit. Grace be with you all."

RECOMMENDED READING LIST

Sonship - A Journey into Father's Heart — M. James Jordan 2012

The Ancient Road Rediscovered — M. James Jordan 2014

The Forgotten Feminine — Denise Jordan 2013

Primal Hope - Finding Confidence Beyond Religion — Stephen Hill 2016

A Father to You — Mark Gyde 2011

Planted in Love — Mark Gyde 2014

The Depth of Love — Mark Gyde 2016

Truth Encounters — Felicia Murrell 2015

River in the Heart — Ingrid Wilts 2011

OTHER BOOKS BY TREVOR GALPIN

Falling from grace into Grace and being caught by the Father — 2012

Jesus and His Father by his family and friends — 2014

Finding the Father in the Story of the Church — 2016

All the above books can be found on Amazon

For more information and resources by Trevor and Linda, please visit:
www.trevorlindafhm.com

www.ingramcontent.com/pod-product-compliance
Lightning Source LLC
Chambersburg PA
CBHW020651300426
44112CB00007B/339